# Politics of Migration

## A Study of Bangladeshis' Refugees

# Politics of Migration
## A Study of Bangladeshis' Refugees

Ashok Kumar Maharana

Delta Book World
New Delhi-110 002

**Politics of Migration: A Study of Bangladeshis' Refugees**
**by Ashok Kumar Maharana**



First Published in 2023
ISBN: 978-81-95911-2-7
Price: ₹ 1295.00



Published by **Abhishek Goel** on behalf of

**Delta Book World**
G-4, Prahlad House
4832/24, Ansari Road
New Delhi - 110 002 (India)

Tel.: 011-4707 2321
E-mail: deltabookworld@gmail.com
Website: www.kaveribooks.com

PRINTED IN INDIA

Dedicated

To

**My Bapa and Maa**

## ACKNOWLEDGEMENTS

I owe a debt of gratitude to almighty God for giving the strength and patience to complete this work.

My father Ramchandra Maharana and mother Sumitra Maharana my living God, are highly thankful for providing me all kinds of moral, intellectual and financial help throughout my work. My elder sister Dr. Sanjukta Maharana, Assistant Professor in Political Science, Government College, Sundargarh, Odisha is specially thankful for providing me all types of academic direction, motivation and suggestions on the basis of which I carried out my research. I am also thankful to all my elder sisters Sabita Maharana and Mamata Maharana and their family and all my nephews whose affection and care infused me all the strength which was essential for me in my academic journey.

Dr. (Mrs) Johani Xaxa, Professor in Political Science, Post Graduate Department of Political Science and Public Administration, is not only my Ph.D. Supervisor, but she is one of my family member whose compassionate and academic direction in my research infused in me the life blood without which the successful completion of this research work would not have been possible at all. Madam has provided me all kinds of academic directions, suggestions and strategies which have been helpful for me in writing this thesis. Madam has also always helped me whenever I found any difficulties and problems in writing this paper. I have no words to give my thanks to my supervisor whose personality and caring nature has always boosted me in my academic work. I sincerely thanks to my supervisor.

Professor Shyama Prasad Guru, my role model in my entire academic journey, I am thankful to him who is a source of inspiration for me. I am also thankful to my teachers Dr. Rajat Kumar Kujur, Dr. Satya Prakash Dash, Dr. Suresh Chandra Patel, Dr. Roshni Kujur, and Dr. Himanshu Sekhar Mishra of Post Graduation Department of Political Science and Public Administration for their valuable direction and help in my research work.

I am specially thankful to Dr. Anjan Kumar Sahu, Assistant Professor, Dept of Public Policy, Law and Governance, School of Social Science, Central University, Rajasthan, who is like my elder brother and whose suggestions have been highly instrumental for me in conducting this work. I am also full of gratitude to my friends who have directly or indirectly provided me a helping hand in completing this work.

**Ashok Kumar Maharana**

# PREFACE

Migration from Bangladesh to India is not new; as the movement of people from East Bengal (the present Bangladesh) to Assam region was started during the British rule in India. The tea industry developed by the British and the necessity of a working class people in Assam paved the way for migration of millions of people to the state. Initially such a movement was never objected either by the Assamese or the people of other parts of India. It was only in the later part of 1970s and throughout 1980s resentment to the migrant people in Assam started. The main organisations which spearheaded the resentment was the All Assam Student's Union (AASU) alleged that the irregular migrants are changing the demography, culture, economy and environment of the Assamese society and hence all the migrants who have illegally staying in Assam should be identified and deported.

Securitisation of the irregular migrants, specifically the Bangladeshi infiltrators, started during the Assam movement of 1970-1985 A.D. In this work, special attentions have been given to unearth the security implications of irregular Bangladeshis' migration in India. Irregular migration is, in fact, a security problem for India. It is the sovereign rights of a responsible country to defend its international border. The Bangladeshi migrants, illegally crossing the country's border, violate the sovereignty of India. India is in the developing state which still struggle to provide a vast section of its people a qualitative life. An additional inflow of people from Bangladesh is a pressure on the country's scarce resources. It has been predicted that millions of Bangladeshis have been successful in entering India and are already settled in many states of the country. Assam is the worst sufferer of the Bangladeshi migration problem since long. There have been many instances of serious law and order problem and violence in Assam. The former Governor of Assam S.K. Sinha, in his letter to the then President of India, has narrated the fact of crisis of identity which Assam is facing due to infiltration of foreign nationals into the region. The Supreme Court of India has also cautioned about the security threat which India is facing due to unabated population infiltration into the state of Assam.

It is not that, all the irregular migrants from Bangladesh are criminals or terrorists but their chance of falling prey in the hands of the anti-India elements and terrorist networks cannot be denied. The terrorists network mainly eyes upon these illiterate migrants for terrorist recruitment and to strengthen the network of Islamic terrorism in India. There are many madrasas which have been setup in Assam by religious fundamentalists where the Muslim migrants of Bangladesh are indoctrinated and are motivated to join terrorist group. This fact has been disclosed by many high level security personnel of India. Moreover, there are many instances of the involvement of these Bangladeshi migrants in drugs trafficking, trafficking of women, girls, weapons, and cows. Thus, it has become a serious headache for Indian Security agencies to deal with such problem in the India-Bangladesh border.

Securitisation of the problem of irregular Bangladeshis' migration in India is the need of time. There is urgent need to devote much energies and resources to control the problem. The problem is not only a threat to the internal security of India but the sovereignty and integrity of India is also in serious danger due to such illegal infiltration at the India-Bangladesh border. It is to be noted that India is a country which has never diminished the human rights of its people. It has also given due reorganisation to the human rights of the foreigners. In the past, India gave asylum to the Dalai Lama and his followers in Himachal Pradesh. The refugees from Pakistan and Bangladesh who suffered religious persecutions back in home have been rehabilitated in India. Thus, while dealing the issue of irregular Bangladeshi migrants in India utmost care is to be given to human rights of the migrants because these people are human being despite their irregular status in India. India-Bangladesh cooperation and political will to solve the problem from both sides of the country can be a positive step in reaching to an amicable solution of the problem.

Overall this work is divided into six chapters. Chapter one introduces the problem of irregular Bangladeshis' migration to India. Chapter two provides for a theoretical frame work to the problem. Chapter three describes the nature and magnitude of irregular migration in India. Chapter four analyses the internal and external security ramification of Bangladeshi migrants who are illegally staying in India. Chapter five provides various solutions to the problem. Chapter six summarises the analysis followed by suggestions for further research.

# CONTENTS

# ABBREVIATIONS

| | | |
|---|---|---|
| AASU | : | All Assam Students' Union |
| AGSP | : | Asom Gana Sangram Parishad |
| AITMC | : | All India Trinomool Congress |
| AJYCP | : | Assam Jatiyatabadi Yuba Chhatra Parishad |
| BBC | : | British Broad Casting |
| BCAS | : | Bangladesh Centre for Advanced Studies |
| BGB | : | Border Guards of Bangladesh |
| BJP | : | Bharatiya Janata Party |
| BoP | : | Border Outpost |
| BNP | : | Bangladesh National Party |
| BSF | : | Border Security Force |
| CCTV | : | Close Circuit Television |
| CPWD | : | Central Public Works Department |
| DC | : | Deputy Commissioners |
| DGFI | : | Director General of Foreign Intelligence |
| DIG | : | Deputy Inspector General |
| ER | : | Electoral Roll |
| EU | : | European Union |
| FICN | : | Figures Fake Indian Currency Notes |
| GDP | : | Gross Domestic Product |
| HUJI | : | Harkat-ul-Jihad-ul-Islami |
| ICJ | : | International Court of Justice |
| IG | : | Inspector General |
| IMDT | : | Illegal Migrants Determination by Tribunals |

IOM : International Organisation for Migration
IPCC : International Governmental Panel on Climate Change
INSAS : Indian Small Arms System
ISI : Inter Service Intelligence
JMB : Jamatul Muzahidin, Bangladesh
MEA : Ministry of External Affairs
MULTA : Muslim United Liberation Tigers of Assam
NBCC : National Buildings Construction Corporation
NDA : National Democratic Alliance
NGO : Non Governmental Organisation
NIA : National Investigating Agency
NTS : Non-Traditional Security
NRC : National Register of Citizens
NREGS : National Rural Employment Guarantee Schemes
NRHM : National Rural Health Mission
NPCC : National Projects Construction Corporation
PIP : Prevention of Infiltration into India of Pakistani Nationals
PIF : Prevention of Infiltration of Foreigners
PWD : Public Works Department
RBI : Reserve Bank of India
RPO : River Police Organisation
RSS : Rashtriya Swayamsevak Sangh
SOP : Standard operating procedure
SP : Superintendent of Police
ULFA : United Liberation Front of Assam
UNDP : United Nations Development Programme
UNHCR : United Nations High Commissioner on Refugees
UN : United Nations
US : United States
VHP : Viswa Hindu Parishad

# 1

# Introduction

After the fall of the Berlin Wall and the subsequent shifting in international environment, a new and broader concept of security began to gain importance in the national security discourse of many countries of the world. This concept of security is very comprehensive which encompasses socio-economic and environmental concerns such as resources scarcity and climate change, water sharing issues, deforestation and forest protection measures, food and health security and large scale population movement from one country to another. Thus the security discourses at present, attempts to build a sustainable and comprehensive security by bringing the state and society together. Before the end of the Cold War, the major referents in the international security were the state and its institutions. Thus security threat at that time was confined to the state i.e. its sovereignty, territorial integrity, and independence. In short, military security was the dominating point in any security measures and discussions at that time. Barry Buzan, a well known security analyst is of the opinion that during the Cold War, mainly three types of security threats were being given importance and those were military threats i.e. seizure of state's territory or damaging the same, invasion, occupation, change of government, and manipulation of policy. The second type of security threat as pointed out by Buzan was the economic threats which were prevailing during the Cold War. It involved attacking the economic structures of a state by another state and consequently destabilising the economic base of the former. And this was materialised through restriction on import and export practices, price manipulations, default on debt, currency control etc. A third category of threat during the Cold War, as pointed out by Buzan, which also revolved round the state, was the ecological security threat. It means damaging the physical base of a state. Buzan is of the opinion that these three types of threats "define (the state's) insecurity, and set the agenda for national security as a security problem"[1]. Again, the state was the main vulnerable institution in the security concern as pointed out by Buzan. So it needed developing state's capabilities in the context of development in military strength of state. In other words it supported for weapon development or armament. It was maintained during the Cold War that if the state's security is ensured then the security of its citizen will necessarily follow. Maintaining balance of power, securing more and more power for a state (the realist point of view on international security), and accumulation of more sophisticated and destructive weapons or maintaining absolute sovereignty for a state was the prime concern during that time.

The security concern as prevalent during the Cold War era or even before that was considered to be Traditional Security concern. In today's world such type of security concern is no more applicable universally and very few states are affected by it. As traditional or military security refers to state's capability to protect itself against outside threats or military attack, war and aggression, it is referred to as state security in contrast to the present notion of human security. Realism, Neo-Realism, Balance of Power theories etc., are some of the international theories on national security where we can notice one thing in common i.e. primacy to nation states. How the state is to become more and more powerful militarily, how the power of a state is to be balanced, how the state will protect itself from military attack etc. were the basic themes in the security theories at that time. It is to be noted that traditional security is also termed as, military or conventional security.

In fact, the traditional security strategies were intended to support only the state's interests and its institutions. The scholars of this school held the view that traditional security aims at protecting a state's boundary, populace, institutions, and their ideals. Protecting a state from external attack was the major issue in that security concern. Walter Lipmann, a well known security analyst, says that state security refers to a state's capacity to prevent or overpower an attack.

The security experts at that time mainly advocated for creating a deterrence so as to prevent any future military threat or attack to the state. So they made use of the strategies of deterrence to sustain the territorial integrity of a state and guard the country from external threats. The traditional notion of security assumes that, as there is no world government to effectively implement global rules and behaviour, it is the responsibility of a state to strengthen itself militarily so that it could protect itself from any military exigencies. It also justifies military preparedness on the ground that, the sovereignty of a state is operating in an anarchical international environment, where there is no adherence to common and universal international laws. In its attempts to strength itself a state mainly relies upon armaments race, alliances or building strategic boundaries. In the state centric view "Security was necessarily understood as concept of equipping oneself with arms and warfare techniques to increase national strength and capability to eliminate threat in the form of foreign aggression and invasion"[2].

The traditional security concern not only emphasises upon external threats which emanates from outside the border but it also emphasises upon threats to the state legitimacy which emanate within the state. These are otherwise known as domestic threats which are open challenges to the legitimacy of the government in power. In this connection internal disturbances are also considered as security issue.

From the above analysis it follows that military power was considered to be the only instrument that can guarantee security to a state. This belief led most of the state during the cold war era to develop military capabilities[3]. The action of one state in developing its own military capabilities was perceived by another state as a probable threat to its security and consequently to arm herself as well. This finally led to Arms Race among states. However, it is to be noted that arms race among the state could not guarantee peace and security for all those states involved in them. When most of the state involves in a competitions to gain more and more military strength then a situation of anarchy and rivalry will follow, as was seen between United States of America and Soviet Union during the Cold War era. So a mad desire to increase their military capacity results in arms race which consequently threatens the security of all. To describe this process Sir Edward Grey said:

"The increase in armaments that is intended in each nation to produce consciousness of strength and a sense of security does not produce these effects. On the contrary, it produces a consciousness of the strength of other nations and a sense of fear. Fear begets suspicion and distrust and evil imagining of all sorts, till each governments feels, that it would be criminal and a betrayal of its own country not to take every precaution, while every governments regards precaution of every government as evidence of hostile intent".

Thus in traditional security concern military strength receives the core attention. It is based on the assumption that higher is the level of military power, greater will be the level of security for a state. Most of the foreign policy makers at that time (during the Cold War era) believed that military strength will ensure them of fulfilling their core national interests.

## Shifting in the Security Concern after the Cold War: From Traditional to Non-Traditional

In this work special attempts have been made to analyse the changing notion of security in the present world. Today the idea of security is very comprehensive and encompassing.

Among the many changes in the international scenario after the cold war world, a significant change has also been noticed in the security concern. The emergence of non-traditional approaches to security is particularly a land mark in the post cold war era of international politics. Many new challenges have started evolving today, which necessitates new and pragmatic efforts for a solution. And as such, the traditional approach to security, based upon the realist school, is now seen as not adequate to fight with emerging security threats. Thus the non-traditional dimension of security is considered as a best approach to understand and analyse the security dilemma in the post cold war period. It is not that the state will completely shift its attention from improving their respective military capabilities and to protect their sovereignty and territorial integrity. In fact, they need to give wider attention to other security challenges. Today security is no longer confined to conventional state centric dimension rather it is very comprehensive and encompasses a much broader connotation.

### Non-Traditional Security: A Comprehensive Security Concern

The idea of a comprehensive national security which emerged in the post cold war era continues even today, and it includes all types of threats to a nation including military and non-military or soft security. "The security in the new world order meant a security that includes protection against all major threats to human survival and well-being and not just military threats. Until now, 'Security' – usually addressed as 'national security' – has meant the maintenance of strong military defence against enemy invasion and attack. These narrow concepts of security have served the state well in the past, when such attack was seen as the only real threat to national survival. Present security encompasses security of resources, environment and threats caused by demographic challenges. The new approach to security believes that security in the new world order should be achieved through defence against severe environmental degradation, worldwide economic crisis, and massive human suffering. Precisely speaking, the non-military threats have become prominent with the flow of globalization, the increasing number of intra-state conflicts, and unprecedented role acquired by the non-state actors. These factors led to the emergence of supplementary approaches to state-centric security in the name of cooperative security, universal security, human security and comprehensive security. During the Cold War and even prior to that, in the interests of 'national security', nation-states were often engaged in a competitive struggle to enhance their own economic and military strength at the expense of other nation's capabilities. This zero sum-competition for security was naturally biased toward unilateral solutions to critical problems. In today's interdependent world, despite certain problems, the quest for security is rapidly becoming a positive-sum process whereby national well being is achieved jointly by all countries"[4].

Unlike the traditional security concern, the present notion of security is a comprehensive one which attempts to ensure security for human being. It tries to protect from all major threats which threatens the survival of human being. Thus not only military threats but also many non military threats are included under the security concern of present world. Today military attack is not seen as only threats to a nation's security and it is even gradually losing its potential to find manifestation in the security discussion with few exceptional cases.

Indeed, the present world encounter with many non-military security threats such as severe environmental pollution and hazards, economic downfall, irregular migration, terrorism, food crisis, drug trafficking and many others. To meet such problems or threats we need universal or collective efforts as no single state alone can be capable of meeting these challenges.

In the changing scenarios of international politics the internal factors are as important as its external factors so far as national security is concerned. In other words, the socio-economic, political, environmental and cultural conditions within the country are equally important along with its military strength. Both the internal and external strength coupled together can lead to a country's wellbeing. So we cannot neglect one at the interest of other. Since competition and conflicts have lost their traditional role, the world needs to divert its attention to non military security concern.

The United Nations played a vital role in initiating the discussion on the non traditional security in the post cold war period. The United Nations Development Programme (UNDP) Report 1994 was a land mark in this direction. The UNDP report primarily emphasises on global initiatives or intellectual discussions on non traditional security or human security. The Copenhagen School is another school of thought which shows active concern on the new or emerging security concern. All these developments in the intellectual and institutional level have necessarily emphasised that "non military issues can be considered as matter of security even if they are not threatening the states"[5] manifestly.

The new security concerns are being given new attention today, which are also called as non military or soft security threats. It is also called as human security as its central focus is on the well being of human being along with state and its institutions. So it is a comprehensive security concern which includes many soft or non military threats. Mely Caballero-Anthony, a security analyst held the view that "These newly emerging threats are referred to as Non-traditional Security (NTS) threats, and they are defined as challenges to the survival and well-being of peoples and states that arise primarily out of non-military sources such as climate change, cross-border environmental degradation and resource depletion, infectious diseases, natural disasters, irregular migration, food shortage, people smuggling, drug trafficking and other forms of transnational crime"[6].

Many countries of the world are now giving due attention to the non traditional security issues in their foreign policy objectives. The Canadian government in 2003, the Japanese government in 2000 gave due attention to the idea of human security and devised plans and programmes to tackle the problem in its foreign policies. It is noted that although military threats still continues to influence the security analysis and discourses, its significance is being declined in comparison to non military security threats and challenges. According to General Rupert Smith "War no longer exists. Confrontation, conflict and combat undoubtedly exist all around the world.... Nonetheless, war as cognitively known to most non-combatants, war as a battle in a field between men and machinery, war as a massive deciding event in a dispute in international affairs– such war no longer exists"[7]. Thus military security threat concern is gradually being diminished as a major area of concern in the security discourses. The above statement given by General Smith essentially reflects a fundamental shift in the security discussion at present. With little exception such statement is applicable to all most all countries of the world today. "In case of India its immediate neighbouring countries Pakistan and China may be interpreted as threat to the security of the country even in the twenty first century. However military action as a deciding factor in a dispute between any of these states is gradually losing its potent mainly due to the possession of nuclear weapons by all the parties. Thus it follows that the military threat perception, even for India, has been fundamentally redefined in the present century"[8]. Thus the traditional military security has been replaced by non military or non traditional security concern. It is also called as human security which is define by the United Nations as "What do we mean by human security? We mean, in its most simple expression, all those things that men and women anywhere in the world cherish most; enough food for the family; adequate shelter; good health; schooling for the children; protection from the violence whether inflicted by man or by nature; and a state which does not oppress its citizens but rules with their consent".

**Irregular Migration as a Security Threat in India**

Among the non traditional or non military threats to the security of a country, irregular migration occupies an important area of concern. Today many states of the world have included irregular migration in their security discourses and are devising policies and programmes to avert this threat. In the context of India, irregular migration from its neighbouring Bangladesh has become a matter of security concern, because since decades there has been continuous flow of migrants to India through illegal means. Even today the Bangladeshi migrants have chosen legal routes to enter India but have subsequently disappeared in the country with no intention to return back. In other words today the Bangladeshis are using new strategies to enter India. The influx of Bangladeshis in to the Indian soil has been resented by the locals and it has even led to serious law and order problems which were manifested in the 1970s and 1980s in Assam and other parts of the country. Upon the arrival of the migrants there have been started a competition between the former and the native people over the resources. When such competition becomes severe and in some cases politicised then it lead to the demand for preservation of local identity, which in turned fuelled violence and jeopardise the internal security of India.

India has been badly affected due to the problem of irregular migration from Bangladesh. Irregular migration is giving severe warning to the internal security of the state. The internal politics of Bangladesh, economic deprivation of the people, coupled with adverse climate impacts are the major factors for such migration. Therefore irregular migration as security challenge has received wider attention today although it was not so considered earlier[9].

Irregular migration from Bangladesh to India can be match

up to the migrants' movement from Mexico to the United States. It has put pressure on India's resource base in the North East and West Bengal. As per some studies Bangladeshi migrants could be around 15 to 20 million all over India. Local resentment to the migrants in the state of Assam has even resulted in a demand for secession from the Indian Union. In Assam, the groups that faces the threats of being demographically overwhelmed by migrants have even go to the extent of arguing that the federal government in New Delhi is unwilling or unable to prevent the irregular migration[10].

Keeping in view all these developments in the security domain of many states around the world, this research is devoted to an inquiry into the emerging security threats to India with specific reference to irregular migration into India from Bangladesh. It is a well known fact that irregular migration is an emerging security problem not only for India, but many developing and developed countries worldwide have suffered a lot due to the population inflow from outside the country.

Thus a central issue in this work is to explore the link between irregular migration and its security implications for India. Since decades, millions of people of Bangladesh have migrated to India due to many factors like political crisis, economic backwardness, high population density and most importantly the rapidly changing climate condition in Bangladesh which have acted as a push factor behind mass migration. Devastating impacts of environment change on cultivation, life and livelihood of an overwhelming number of people of Bangladesh have derailed their source of income and hence threatened their very existence. Bangladesh is prone to frequent floods, cyclones and severe droughts due to its geographical location. And in the face of rapid changes in climate condition all these extreme climate events are likely to be multiplied in future. Therefore as an adaptive measure to the problem, it is predicted that many Bangladeshi people will be forced to migrate towards India in the coming days.

Migration from Bangladesh is not new and it has its root to the pre-colonial period. Moreover Rapid changes in the climate condition of Bangladesh will add to the on-going pattern of migration to India. Sanjoy Hazarika and Ashok Swain, two scholars are of the opinion that the increasing environmental destruction in Bangladesh force people to migrate to neighbouring country to find work and livelihood. As per the study of the Bangladesh Centre for Advanced Studies (BCAS), about 17.5 per cent of the entire land area will be submerged and 11 per cent of the populace will be banished if there takes place a meter increase in the sea level and hence the consequence will be searching for alternative places to settle.

There are many push factors behind mass migration from Bangladesh to India and this research work focuses on all the factors responsible for such mass migration. India is already flooded with Bangladeshi migrants and it is unearthed by many agencies that around 15-20 million Bangladeshi migrants are staying illegally in various parts of India and majority of them are found in Assam, West Bengal and Tripura. The push factor behind it is not only the changing climate but many socio-economic and political factors works behind it. An eminent scholar S. Alam once observed that shortage of land and water in rural areas due to increase population, climate change, uneven distribution of resources and developmental works in Bangladesh is resulting in serious unemployment, shortage of land for living and agriculture, destabilisation in wage structure etc., which is consequently forcing many people to illegally enter into India. Another scholar Myers says that due to climate change millions of affected people will come from Bangladesh to India; 26 million migrants will leave Bangladesh in the coming days.

The migrants mainly chose to enter India through illegal route or clandestinely because the cost of hiring visas cannot be afforded by most of them due to their poverty. Moreover they also show unwillingness to fulfil the legal procedure to come to India. So they opt for the short cut route i.e. to cross the border illegally which they think, free of cost and non burdensome. As India-Bangladesh border is very porous and there are certain areas which cannot be protected through fencing, it helps them to infiltrate into India. There are also some touts who facilitates such illegal entry to India in return of some money. It is to be noted that the dignity of Border Security Force (BSF) of India cannot be questioned who are protecting the long India-Bangladesh border very effectively since many decades. However, there are very few cases where the border guarding forces are involved in such illegal migration in collusion with the tout. The reasons behind migration from Bangladesh are varied and a multiple of socio-economic, political and environmental factors acts as push factor of such migration. When we analyse the history of Assam it is found that, being influenced by the development of tea industry in Assam by an Assamese aristocrat named Maniram Dutta Barua the British started hiring labour from the East Bengal to Assam at that time. Because there was shortage of labour to work in the tea garden and the vacuum was fulfilled by the East Bangladeshi workers. And that trend continued and it got political support when Sir Syed Sadaullah came to power in Assam. Mr. Sadaullah wanted to convert Assam into a Muslim majority region and in the name of grow more food scheme he encouraged millions of Muslims to come to Assam and settle there. The situation was taken full advantage by the people of east Bengal and there started continuous influx of population to the Assam region. After the independence of India, many people from East Pakistan (present Bangladesh) came to India due to religious persecution. Such a population influx was, however, considered as sons and daughters of the country coming home. It was after the India-Pakistan war of 1965, migration from East Pakistan was looked with utmost seriousness. Migration of people from East Pakistan became severe when the Pakistani Army resorted to the killing of all those people who were involved in the civil war there. The civil war resulted in mass slaughter, and around two million people in Bangladesh at that time were assassinated and two lakhs girls and women were mistreated. Moreover, about 10 million people were forced to cross the international border and took refuge in India. The genocide perpetrated by the Pakistani army forced millions of people to migrate especially to India. Poverty and economic backwardness in Bangladesh is another push factor behind mass migration to India. These are those sections of people who did not leave their country due to religious persecution or state atrocities but they have come for economic reason i.e. to escape from gruelling poverty and backwardness and they are not refugees but are called as Irregular Migrants. In fact irregular migration from Bangladesh still continues and it has been observed that, there are approximately 15-20 millions Bangladeshis residing illegally in various parts of India.

Resentment to the Bangladeshi migration started in Assam in the late 1970s. The 1961 population Census revealed that a big quantity of East Pakistani people, mainly Muslims, had entered Assam illegally. The All Assam Students' Union (AASU) and Asom Gana Sangram Parishad (AGSP) started a state wide agitation to detect and deport all the foreigners staying illegally in Assam. These two organisations alleged that the migrants are influencing the demography, economy and culture of the Assamese society. They also feared that Assam is under serious demographic invasion and is facing crisis of identity due to heavy population influx from Bangladesh. Subsequently the agitation took violent character where thousands of people were dead. Considering the seriousness of the situation, Mrs. Indira Gandhi, the then Prime Minister of India decided to interfere on the issue. Later on it was due to the effort of the subsequent Prime Minister Mr. Rajeev Gandhi, the famous Assam Accord was signed between the AASU, the Union Government and the Assam Government which halted the agitation. As per the Assam Accord, all the foreigners from

Assam will be identified through the implementation National Register of Citizens (NRC). Then the process of identification of the foreigners started to detect the foreigners. However the process could not proceed due to resentment of many Muslim people supported by some political parties. It was alleged that central government is harassing the indigenous Muslim in the name of the NRC. They alleged that, as we are staying in Assam since decades why we should prove our identity. Keeping in view all the situation in mind, the central government directed that the process of identification should be properly done which slowed down the entire process. After more than three and half decades the Bharatiya Janata Party (BJP) led by National Democratic Alliance (NDA) came to power in the centre and in its election campaign in Assam it had declared that all the irregular Bangladeshi infiltrators from Assam will be identified and deported back to Bangladesh. Subsequently, under the direction and supervision of the Supreme Court of India the process of NRC was completed in Assam where the name of around nineteen lakhs people are missing from the final NRC list. It is to be noted that in the absence of proper mechanism and the bilateral agreement with Bangladesh government it seems impossible to deport such millions of people from Assam. Moreover due to some mistakes in the final list of NRC the central government has asked them to prove their citizenship by filling petition in tribunals set up for this purpose. So all these developments in Assam makes it clear that Bangladeshi migrants are found to be present in large number who have migrated to India due to combination of several factors.

Initially, migration from Bengal during the British rule in India was mainly due to economic reason. Subsequently the intention to convert Assam into a Muslim majority region by some vested interest groups in India encouraged mass migration into Assam region. Political persecution and state atrocities also forced millions of people to leave the country. Again religious intolerance and violence in Bangladesh is another factor which has forced millions of Hindus to leave the country. It is to be noted that migration of Muslim population who fled the country not because of religious atrocities but because of economic reason is seriously objected in India. Again, many pull factors in India has facilitated the migration of Bangladeshi people to many Indian states. The porous border, better employment opportunities, vote bank politics, presence of vested interest groups, better education and health care system and more important, the secular-democratic character of India has attracted millions of Bangladeshis to enter India illegally.

Irregular migration from Bangladesh is objectionable due to its security implications for India. In other words, such migration from Bangladesh has negatively influenced the demography, economy, culture and the security of India. It is the duty of every responsible government to protect its international border from illegal infiltration. And the migrants by illegally crossing the border of India go against the sovereignty of India. Again, their involvement in many anti-social and anti-Indian activities is seriously threatening the internal security of India. There are many instances where the migrants have already encroached the government land, forest land and land belonging to reserved sanctuaries in Assam. They have also changed the local economy and wage structure in Assam. Competition with the locals in job markets has also left many locals jobless in Assam. As the migrants are ready to work in difficult situation and even relatively low prices, the contractors prefer them to the local Assamese. At present, these migrants have organised into groups and there are many instances of violence with the locals.

Another central issue in this research work is to discover the security implications of climate change induced migration. Among other factors, climate change induced migration has caused and will intensify strain on the natural and other resources in the country accepting migrants. In the context of

India the country is already under increasing population with rising expectation. The infrastructure in the country is yet to fully support the needs of its increasing population. An additional flow of people will, therefore, create further pressure and affect the capacity of the state to meet the need of its people. Assam, a North-East State of India has witnessed a number of strife between migrants of Bangladesh and the people of local tribes. The All Assam Student's Union started a movement in the late 1970s with the demand of identification and deportation of all unauthorised Bangladeshi migrants staying in Assam. Their demands rested on the ground that the migrants are influencing economy, security, political system and local demographic structure. Till 1985 the Assam movement continued and caused up to 7,000 deaths of human life. In the year 2018, the publication of the draft NRC report in the state of Assam clearly highlights the fact that millions of Bangladeshis are living in the state of Assam.

Few years back a conflict arose between Bodo tribe and the Muslim community in Assam. When the movement was halted the Bodo began to blame the unauthorised Bangladeshis for their involvement in the incident which resulted in 100 deaths and displacement of 4,00,000 who fled to the relief camps in the area. As of October 2012, around 1,33,000 people were still in the relief camps which once again remind us the 1985 conflict in Assam. Though migration in India has been going on almost a hundred years it is only for the last three decades that irregular migration from Bangladesh to Assam came in the frontline as triggering factor behind group conflict, between native and the migrants. Not only confined to the state of Assam, Bangladeshis have also penetrated to all most all states of India including West Bengal, Maharashtra, Rajasthan, Tamil Nadu, Delhi, Gujarat and Odisha. Therefore the Union Minister of Home Affairs Mr. Amit Shah informed the Rajya Sabha on November 2019 that NRC will be implemented throughout the country.

It has been observed that, many Muslim migrants from Bangladesh have been settled in the state of Assam. They have even formed an organisation known as 'Assam Liberation Army' which recruits from the fresh migrants. The Hindustan Times (New Delhi), 20$^{th}$ December 1992 reported that at the time of post-Ayodhya communal violence in India in December 1992, in the Nagaon district of Assam, the Muslim migrants under the 'AMLA' were strong enough to engineer a brutal massacre evidently to drive out Hindus from their land. Most of the migrants are settled in Nagaon, Darrang, Barpeta and Kamrup district in close proximity to each other and are organised against threats from the native community.

In 1995 Professor Ashok Swain an eminent scholar made a visit to the Bengalipura area of Mumbai. Interviews with the local residents confirmed the presence of nearly 50,000 Bangladeshi migrants in the slum areas. According to them Bangladeshi Muslim migrants in the locality have started organising themselves to counter discrimination and possible deportation and the situation may lead to a violent conflict in the near future.

The migrants, coming from Bangladesh, have also penetrated into Delhi, the National Capital of India. In 1993, in his interview with the migrants at the place Prof. Ashok Swain found that 1,00,000 Bangladeshi Muslim migrants were living in slum colonies near Yamuna river in Delhi. Swain interviewed six Muslim migrants in their slums in Delhi who were very apprehensive of their future. All had come to Delhi in 1980s from the south-western part of Bangladesh, four due to lose of agriculture and two due to river bank erosion. They also admitted the fact of organising them into group so as to avert any threat to their existence in the areas. The security ramification of irregular migration once again received wider attention in 1993 when the senior officials of Central Reserve Police and the India Army alleged that Pakistani Intelligence agency is successful in recruiting its agents from among irregular Bangladeshi to create disturbances in the North-East. The former Governor of Assam R.K Sinha, in his report to the then President of India, expressed serious concern to the problem of illegal migration in Assam. In his report the Governor said that Assam is now facing serious crisis of identity. The demography of Assam is changing in a rapid pace and a day will come that the local Assamese will be a minority in their own land due to heavy influx of foreigners. The Supreme Court of India has also expressed concern over the problem. The former Chief of Army General Bipin Rawat also stated that every day thousands of Bangladeshi nationals are entering into India and there number could cross millions.

The growth of madrasas along the Indo-Bangladesh border inside India and the growth of a number of villages confirm the fact of continuous population influx to Assam. The migrants are mostly illiterate people and hence fall prey in the hands of many criminal gangs. These people are used by these gangs in giving effect to their criminal action. Due to allurement of easy money these migrants are involved in many criminal activities. They are involved in crimes like theft, trafficking of drugs, cow, arms and weapons. Moreover, conflicts with the local tribal and Assamese due to competition over resources is the biggest threat to the internal security of Assam. The hidden plan of Pakistan's Inter Service Intelligence (ISI) to convert Assam into a Muslim region through population influx form Bangladesh is also clear. Most of the madrasas set up in the border districts of Assam are mainly involved in the indoctrination of these migrants. Many Islamic fundamentalists of Bangladesh have made their entry into Assam and are even successful in obtaining land and houses there. These fundamentalist elements mainly inculcate the feeling of religious bitterness among their students against the Indian states. In most of the cases many terrorist group recruit people for terrorist activities from the migrants stock. It is not that all the Bangladeshi migrants are criminals or are becoming terrorists but the fact of their easy indoctrination cannot be ignored. As most of them are illiterate and very poor they fall prey in the hands of the anti-Indian elements.

Mere analysis of the problem of irregular Bangladeshis' migration to India is not going to solve the problem. At the same time there is necessity of analysing the existing policies and initiatives undertaken by the Indian government followed by certain recommendations which could bring a solution to the current problem which the country is facing. Since the partition of India in 1947 the country has tried to deal with the problem and the Government of India took several steps to discourage the migrants to enter into India. Reservation of land for the tribal of Assam, Enactment of Immigrants (Expulsion from Assam) Act of 1950, Prevention of Infiltration into India of Pakistani Nationals (PIP) scheme, creation of the Foreigner's Tribunal under Clause 2 of the Foreigners (Tribunal) Order on September 23, 1964, illegal migrants (Determination by Tribunals) IMDT Act etc. are some important measures. Moreover, fencing of the India-Bangladesh border, installation of better surveillance system, increasing the border patrolling by the border guarding forces are certain important measures which have been adopted by the Government of India. However, all these measures have not been able to completely eradicate the problem and there is need to devise new strategies or improvising the exiting measures for a better solution of the problem. Keeping in view the existing scenario, in this research work several relevant suggestions have been made which can be helpful for the researchers and policy makers to find a better solution.

In a nutshell, the present research work aims at exploring the changing notion of security concern in the post-cold war era. Moreover, attempts have been made to discuss the security implications of irregular Bangladeshis' migration in the context of India, followed by an analysis of the causes of such migration. Again, certain suggestions have also been made followed by an analysis of the bilateral agreements between

India and Bangladesh to solve the problem.

Thus the security implications of irregular Bangladeshis' migration cannot be underestimated and there is need to undertake extensive research which could explore the migration-security linkage in the context of India. In a nutshell, in this research it is intended to establish the close relationship that exists between irregular Bangladeshis' migration and the security domain of India. Irregular migration is definitely a security problem for the country and it is high time to take adequate steps to meet the problem. It has already pressurised the demography, economy, culture of Assam and has also caused several law and order problems and violent conflicts in several states of India. Assam, West Bengal, Delhi, Mumbai and many North Eastern states are seriously affected by this problem. In the changing environment of security concern it is high time to securities irregular Bangladeshis' migration without ignoring the human rights of the migrants and there is the necessity to devote much energies and effort to meet this emerging security threat to India.

Keeping in view the emerging security concern i.e. irregular migration and its security implications, several authors have made valuable intellectual contribution on the subject. There are many factors responsible behind irregular migration from Bangladesh to India, and in this research work it is intended to highlight all those factors through rigorous analysis of many relevant literatures. Moreover there is deficient of research papers which specifically interlink climate induced migration from Bangladesh to India and its impact on peace and security of India. Thus through this research work it is also intended to find out several climate factors in Bangladesh which have been responsible for mass migration to India. Several materials such as articles from journals, government reports, news paper publications, and findings of many research work conducted by many research organisations have been studied analysed for the present work.

In his article entitled "*The New Global Citizen is Seeking New Roots*" Ravi Shankar (2018), has clearly mentioned about the security implications of irregular Bangladeshi migrants in India. Regarding the number of irregular Bangladeshi infiltrators in India, the author has referred to the statement of government of India in 2004 where the government stated in Parliament that there are 1.2 crore illegal Bangladeshi infiltrators living in India, and three lakh are being added every year. West Bengal is the host with the 5.7 million. The author has also mentioned the estimates made by the then government, which holds that the number of irregular Bangladeshis in India is around two crore. So far as the security implications these infiltrators on Indian territory is concerned, the author is of the opinion that the migrants upset the prevailing wage structure as they are agree to work in low price, they also clear forest and set up illegal colonies and also work the corrupt system to get domicile documents. He also clearly narrated about how the illegal madrasas along the West Bengal-Bangladesh border operated by maulvis of dubious national loyalty could threaten India's national security. Because these madrasas are acting as breeding ground of Islamist intolerance and terrorism and are often acting as safe houses for ISI infiltrators.

The book entitled "*Operation Lebensraum: Illegal Migration from Bangladesh*" written by Mr Hiranya Kumar Bhattacharya (2018) is one of the outstanding work for the students undertaking research on irregular Bangladeshis' migration to India. In this book the author has given a clear description about the problem of irregular migration in Assam. This book not only gives a clear cut picture on the historical background of the problem but also highlights the present trend of Bangladeshi migration. Most important, in this book the author has interlinked irregular Bangladeshis' migration to the national security of India. In other words the security ramification of irregular migration for the country India is the most important area of discussion of the book. In the last part of his work the author has also analysed about several measures adopted by the Government of India to meet the problem.

In his famous book entitled "*Bangladesh Migration: A Threat to India*" the author P.K. Mishra (2014), has not only described about several causes of Irregular Bangladeshi migration to the state of Assam but also described about its security implications for India. How the infiltrators are being used by the fundamentalists and terrorist organisation to create security problem in India is clearly discussed in this book. In this book the author has narrated his practical experiences gained during his working as a top ranking Indian security officer at the India-Bangladesh border area for a long period. At the final section of the book the author has come with several suggestions to deal with the problem. In a nut shell, the book is an outstanding work as it gives an in depth knowledge regarding the problem of irregular Bangladeshi migration problem in India.

Pushpita Das (2016) in her outstanding work entitled "*Illegal Migration from Bangladesh: Deportation, Border Fences and Work Permits*" clearly narrates the causes of migration from Bangladesh to India. In this work the author has described about the migration pattern from East Bengal to Assam from the colonial period to the 21st century India. Here, the author has not only linked irregular Bangladeshi migration to the security and territorial integrity of India but has also given several suggestions to solve the problem. The critical analysis of several measures undertaken by the government of India to meet the problem is the most attractive area of discussion of this paper. In short this paper can be a well accepted work among the scholars and policy makers to have a clear cut understanding about a new security threat which India is facing.

In his famous article entitled "*Illegal Bangladeshi Migration: Evaluating India-Bangladesh Approaches*" Sanjay Bhardwaj (2014) is of the opinion that, the movement of people from one place to another leaving their original residence can be a strategy to adapt themselves with the changing socio-economic and environment structure of the country of origin. In this article Mr. Bhardwaj gives a clear picture on the historical background of migration from the present Bangladesh to Indian states. The author is of the opinion that, it was only after the creation of Bangladesh in 1971 that those who migrated from there began to be considered as illegal. He has also quoted the report of the Group of Minister (GOM) which says that there are around 15 million Bangladeshi nationals who have migrated illegally and settled in different parts of India. Mr. Bhardwaj has also listed various causes of migration from Bangladesh and has also linked migration to the security of India. In the final section of the paper the author has given useful suggestions to meet the problem. This work is one of the unique contribution to the study of irregular migration from Bangladesh to India.

In his book entitled "*Climate Change and Its Security Aspects: Threatening the Food Security of India*" Ashok Kumar Maharana (2017), has described about the fundamental shift that has been taken place in the security concern after the end of the cold war in international politics. In this book the author has specifically described about the security implications of climate change. Moreover he has discussed about the adverse impacts of climate change on the food security of India in particular. However little is known about the irregular Bangladeshis' migration to India.

In his famous article entitled "*Concepts of Security Threats, Challenges, Vulnerabilities and Risks*", Hans Gunter Brauch (2011) has done a commendable work in so far as security studies and analysis is concerned. The author, in this article, has clearly narrated about the various concepts like Security, Challenges and Threats, which enhance our understanding on fundamental concepts in security studies. The pattern of security concern during the cold war or even before, followed by an inquiry into the changes in the security paradigm after cold war has been thoroughly discussed in this work. How many countries of the world are giving renewed concern to the non traditional security threats in their defence papers is another area of discussion in this article. However little is known regarding the irregular migration from Bangladesh to India from this paper.

Subhakanta Behera (2011) in his research paper entitled "*Trans-border Identities: A study on the impact of the Bangladeshi and Nepali migration to India*" has described about the pattern of migration to India from the adjoining neighbours Bangladesh and Nepal. This paper discusses about the causes of such migration followed by its impact on the security domain of India. Finally this paper concludes with brief suggestions to deal with the problem. Thus, the research work is highly valuable to understand how irregular migration is an emerging security threat for India.

In the paper entitled "*Implications of the Securitisation of Migration*" Elisabeth Farny (2016), has specifically mentioned about US's response to the problem of irregular migration. How US changed its perception to the problem of migration in the country after 9/11 terrorist attack is clearly illustrated in this paper. This paper proves worthy for the scholars and policy makers who are studying the history of securitisation of irregular migration in the world. However, little is known about the problem of irregular migration in India from this work.

In his article entitled "*Irregular migration, state security and human security*" Khalid Koser (2005) has not only described about the impact of irregular migration on the security of receiving state but also described about the problems faced by the migrants themselves in the receiving state. He said that the process exposes both the destination country and the migrants to insecurity and vulnerability. In this paper the author has also given some relevant suggestions to solve the problem of irregular migration. To him, it requires "more effective and coherent approaches to address the issue of irregular migration that recognises the concerns of the states in this respect and the need to protect the rights of irregular migrants".

In his article entitled "*Reshaping India's National Security in the Face of Irregular Bangladeshi Migration to India: Search for Possible Solutions*" Ashok Kumar Maharana (2018) has clearly mentioned about the security threats which India is facing as a result of migrants influx from Bangladesh. The author in this paper has highlighted the need to reshape the security concerns of India in this changing scenario. If such challenges are ignored now, then there will be no time left to address the problem except to face its disastrous consequences. Most important, in this article certain valuable suggestions have been made to solve this emerging security challenge to India.

In his article entitled "*Beginning and Endings*" Udayon Misra (2018) has described about the publication of draft NRC (National Register of Citizens) by the Assam government in August 2018. In this article the author has recalled the preparedness of the Assam government to deal with any possible violence or disturbances which would take place as a reaction to the publication NRC report. Thanks to the gentleness of the people, who are not registered in the NRC, not a single case of violence was noticed in the state after the draft publication of the NRC in 2018. He also clearly mentions about the threat to Assamese language due to the presence of a large number of irregular Bangladeshi infiltrators in the state. In a nut shell this article is a commendable work to understand the problem of irregular Bangladeshi infiltrators and its consequences.

In his famous article, "*Illegal Migration from Bangladesh: Threat to India's Internal Security*", N. Manoharan (2014) has clearly discussed about several socio-political disturbances in Bangladesh which have forced many people to migrate to India.

Moreover in this article the author has discussed about the security problems created by these migrant population in India.

In his article named, "*Illegal Immigration from Bangladesh to India: Toward a Comprehensive Solution*", Sanjeev Tripathi (2016) has done a noteworthy research in describing the figures of migrants from Bangladesh who are illegally staying in different parts of India. In this article the author has critically analysed the existing legal frame work and policies in India to meet the problem of illegal Bangladeshi infiltration. Furthermore Mr. Tripathy has also highlighted about the importance of bilateral agreement between India and Bangladesh to solve the problem. However, so far as the security implication of these migrants for India is concerned, very little is known from this article.

The work of Joyeeta Bhattacharjee (2014), entitled "*India: Resolving the Bangladesh Immigration Issue*" is an outstanding contribution in understanding the problem of Bangladeshi migration in India. In this work the author has opined that India-Bangladesh bilateral discussion can be a positive step to prevent the infiltrators from crossing the international border.

The article entitled "*Understanding the Historical Conflicts Behind Today's Violence in Assam*" written by Arpita Bhattacharyya (2012) gives a clear cut picture on the historical background of the conflict and violence in Assam. Several recent instances of violence and conflicts between the indigenous Assamese people have also been discussed in this paper, which is very informative to understand the security environment of Assam. Moreover, in this article the author is of the opinion that climate change in Bangladesh will displace millions of people of the country.

Hiranya K. Nath and Suresh Kr. Nath (2010) in their joint research work entitled "*Illegal Migration into Assam: Magnitude, Causes, and Economic Consequences*" describes about diverse facets of illegal movement of people into Assam from Bangladesh. In this article the authors are of the opinion that increasing population in Bangladesh with lower employment opportunity has forced thousands of people of Bangladesh to move towards Assam where the chances of obtaining land for residence and agriculture and economic opportunity is higher. The positive impacts of migrants in Assam society also find manifestation in this paper. How the migrants provide a cheap source of labour in Assam, their new techniques of cropping, their working skills etc have been discussed in this paper. Moreover, the authors have also stated that the migrants have seriously pressurised the land sector which causes adverse effects on the economy of India. In a nut shell, this paper proves very beneficial for the students undertaking research on the impacts of migrants on the Assam society.

Pranati Datta (2004) in her article entitled "*Push-Pull Factors of Undocumented Migration from Bangladesh to West Bengal: A Perception Study*" says that about 15 million Bangladeshi migrants illegally living in India. In this paper, the author has highlighted on several push and pull factors which influence migration from Bangladesh to India. The author has stated that a combination of economic, demographic and security factors have forced millions of Bangladeshi nationals to move to India illegally. She also stated that "the economic push factors that motivate people to leave Bangladesh are instability and economic depression, poverty, lack of employment opportunity, struggle for livelihood, forced grabbing of landed property from minority group, and lack of industrialization in Bangladesh". Demographic factors such as higher population growth and low development rate are forcing people to migrate to India. In this paper the author has done a commendable job in highlighting the causes of irregular migration which enables the students to undertake further research on this field.

The work of J Das and D Talukdar (2016) entitled "*Socio-*

*Economic and Political Consequence of Illegal Migration into Assam from Bangladesh*" is highly praiseworthy as it highlights the negative consequences of irregular Bangladeshi migration on the socio-economic domain of Assam. The authors have held the view that Assam is facing the crisis of identity due to uncontrolled population infiltration from Bangladesh. The socio-political and environmental condition of Assam is in serious danger due to the ongoing phenomena. The authors have also highlighted the fact that how political supports to the irregular migrants in Assam have made the situation more complicated and it also creates obstacles in finding solutions to the problem. The authors have portrayed the irregular migration problem as a threat to the security of India and hence they have given some relevant suggestions to solve the problem.

Ashish Dwivedi (2018) in his article entitled "*Threat of Illegal Bangladeshis to India's national security and political stability*" has shown serious concern about the continuous infiltration in the India-Bangladesh border. He is of the opinion that as many as fifty Bangladeshis are entering into India every day. This observation of the author clearly highlights the intensity of illegal infiltration at the border which poses a serious security threat for India. In this article the author says that political support to the migrants in India has encouraged further migration. The work of the author is highly praiseworthy as it helps in obtaining a sound knowledge to the irregular migration problem in India.

Nikhil Raj Aggarwal (2019), in his research article entitled "*The Threat of a Revitalised JMB to India's Security*" clearly mentions the security threat which India is facing due to illegal infiltration from Bangladesh. The modus operandi of the terrorist organisation in terrorist recruitment from the irregular migrants finds manifestation in this paper. And in this connection of the author has discussed the role of Jamaat ul Mujahideen Bangladesh (JMB), a terrorist organisation which recruits fresh terrorist form the migrant stock. However, the author has not given any historical interpretation to the migration from Bangladesh and his study is limited in establishing a link between irregular migration and national security of India.

In an article entitled "*Illegal Migration in Assam: A Concern for India's National Security*" the author Namrata Goswami (2006) has described about the security implications that illegal migration will create for Assam. The author says that illegal migration in Assam is the greatest security threat for India. How Bangladeshi migration to Assam assumed political and communal overtones after independence, and continues to be an issue of concern even today is clearly presented in this paper. In short, this article is a systematic study on the problem of Bangladeshi migration into Assam and its link to the security of India.

In his article entitled "*Illegal Bangladeshi Migration to India: Impact on Internal Security*" Anand Kumar (2010) states that Illegal Bangladeshi Migrants are also threat to language and culture of Assam. The hidden intention of Pakistan's ISI to convert Assam into a volatile region is analysed in this article. Moreover, the author says that the illegal migrants are not involved into terrorism in a big way, but are involved in gun running, running of fake currency rackets and drug trafficking. The author has done a commendable work in describing about the internal and external security threats which India is facing due to Bangladeshi migration.

In the research paper entitled, "*Displacing the conflict: environmental destruction in Bangladesh and ethnic conflict in India*" Ashok Swain (1996), has given a clear picture of the link between irregular Bangladeshi migrants and India's national security. In his article he is of the opinion that the Bangladeshi Muslim migrants have started organising themselves to counter discrimination and possible deportation which may lead to violent conflict in the near future.

In an article entitled "*Its time countries took climate-linked migration seriously*", William Lacy Swing has discussed about the changing climate conditions and its impact on mankind which forces many affected people to seek to other places for their survival. In the middle part of the article William Lacy Swing has related two phenomena i.e. climate change induced migration and possible conflict in the receiving areas due to competition over resources i.e. land, water, jobs etc. In the final part of the article the author has also given certain suggestions for bringing about solution to the emerging problem. However, in this paper the author has not given any information regarding irregular Bangladeshis' migration to India.

Neil Padukone in a paper entitled "*Climate change in India: Forgotten Threats, Forgotten Opportunities*", is of the opinion that climate change is going on and its impacts are already noticed in India. Here the author has brought into light several adverse impact of climate change in India that starts from food insecurity, migration, water conflict, resource stress and conflict etc. In the final section of this paper the author has warned mankind about the negative impact of climate change which if not addressed, then there will be left no time but to see the future devastation of human life. However, in this article little is known about the irregular migration.

The study of Kate Burrows and Patrick Kinney summarised in their work, "*Exploring the Climate Change, Migration and Conflict Nexus*", is noteworthy as it establishes a link between climate change-migration on the one hand and migration-conflict on the other hand. An important thing that has been highlighted in this paper is the non-seriousness to climate change impacts and its consequences. The authors are of the opinion that climate change is going on and it will increase the climate extremes. Although some scholars differ in their opinion with regard to the impact of climate change, it cannot be denied that the impact of climate change upon human life is dangerous.

In his work "*Climate Induced Migration from Bangladesh to India: Issues and Challenges*", Architesh Panda (2016) has made a rigorous study to discover the problem of climate change in Bangladesh and how it is forcing the affected people to migrate to India. He is of the opinion that climate refugees will create many destabilising socio-political and economic impacts in future. Currently thousands of people continue to move into India from Bangladesh due to many social-economic and cultural factors. Moreover climate change and environmental pressure will complicate the problem by forcing more people to migrate to India. Mr. Panda again observe that the determinants of migration from Bangladesh to India can be historical and cultural ties, regional and linguistic similarities and greater economic opportunities in India. However, in this paper little efforts have been made to specify the security impacts, generated due to the presence of climate migrants of Bangladesh in India.

In their joint work "*Climate Change, Migration and Conflict in South Asia*", Arpita Bhattacharya and Michael Werz (2012) are of the opinion "that climate change will increase resource conflicts within and among countries, increase migration pressures on hundreds of millions of people, increase the number of humanitarian disasters and disrupt the economies all over the world and threaten military preparedness". To them, climate change increase resource scarcity in the affected areas and may lead to conflict directly or may foster migration causing group conflict in the receiving places which may be within their own country or outside. This article is highly relevant for those undertaking research on migration and conflict issue. Several conflicts and clashes between people of receiving areas and migrants from Bangladesh have been discussed in this paper. The security implications of irregular Bangladeshi's migration in the state of Assam have been the main area of discussion of this work. The author has recalled a conflict in Assam which took place 1980 where "a group called the All Assam Student's Union began a movement calling for the deportation of all supposed unauthorised Bangladeshi migrants saying that the migrants were influencing their economy, security and political system".

In his classic work "*Concepts of Security Threats, challenges, vulnerabilities and Risks*", Hans Gunter Brauch (2011) is of the opinion that military threats have disappeared since the end of East-West conflict in 1990 and thus the threat perception has fundamentally changed. The author in this work has discussed about the changing conception of security threat. He holds that the classic threat concept i.e. military threat lost its importance, and the security concept includes various new dimensions such as economic, societal and environmental. Specifically highlighting about climate change as a security threat, Brauch has mentioned a statement of Gorbachev, former General Secretary of the Communist Party of the Soviet Union. In 1988 Gorbachev held that "The relationship between man and environment has become menacing". "The threat from the sky is no longer missile but global warming". But in this article little work is done to establish the link between irregular migration and security of a country.

In a paper entitled "*India's Non-Traditional Security Concerns*", Ms. Puseletso Nkopane (2013) has elaborately discussed about the fundamental shift that has been taken place in the nature of security threat in the entire world in general and India in particular. Here the author is of the opinion that "the concept of national security is no longer strictly confined to traditional state centric security concerns predominantly focused on external threats but now embraces alternative approaches that aim to address fundamental challenges to human security in a given state". Here the author has done a commendable work by specially mentioning about the non-traditional security threats of India. Under this new type of threat concept, Ms. Nkopane has included climate change, food security, irregular migration and many others new challenges that threatens the survival and well-being of peoples and the states.

In the article entitled "*Defining Non-Traditional Security Threats*", published by Global India Foundation, Mr. Saurabh Chaudhuri has highlighted about several non-traditional security threats which has been given due importance in the security discourses in the year following the end of the Cold War. It examines about six broad branches of non-traditional security challenges namely international terrorism, transnational organised crime, illegal migration, energy security, human security and more importantly environmental security. Moreover, credit goes to the author of this paper in highlighting several measures to deal with such threats. According to the author of this article, "non-traditional security threats are more intimidating than the traditional one which requires the national leadership not only to cultivate international cooperation but also to undertake socio-economic and political reforms". More importantly, this article has highlighted about the new facet of security which emerged since 1991 with the process of globalization, environmental degradation, and international terrorism. In the discourse of political science the nature of security is constantly changing and this expanding security agenda has gone beyond state and military security and hence one need to define security threat in a comprehensive manner.

In a paper entitled "*Traditional and Non-Traditional threats in a changing global order: An Indian perspective*", Ruchita Beri (2007) provides an important insight into the changing nature of security threat which emerged after the end of Cold War. In this paper the author has challenged the state-oriented conventional defence or security study which was the defining concept throughout the Cold War period. According to the author, traditional notion of security refers to the capacity of a state to defend its interests from outside threats and such interests are generally defined as territorial integrity, sovereignty, and independence of a nation. In the changing international environment the danger to the security of a state not only emanates from another state but also from a variety of non-state basis of insecurity. So the author has felt the urgent need to expand the traditional notion of security to address the non-traditional threats and to develop a more comprehensive approach to security because traditional security paradigm do not address the rapidly growing non-traditional threats to security such as energy security, ecological degradation, forced migration, global terrorism or violence and so on.

In their work "*Climate change, human security and violent conflict*", Jon Barnett and W. Neil Adger (2007) have clearly pointed out that "climate change poses risk to human security principally through its adverse effects on people's well-being". In this paper, the authors have given important information regarding the close link that exists between climate change and human security. The authors are of the opinion that climate change undermine human security in the present time and will increasingly do so in future. It threatens human security mainly through reducing people's access to natural resources that are important to sustain their livelihoods.

In a paper entitled "*Factors Influencing Migration and Population Movements*" Mervyn Piesse (2014), has described about the major determinants of irregular migration. In this connection the author has mentioned about various pull and push factors responsible for migration to the destination country. In fact, this paper enriches our understanding on the factors driving migration from the country of origin to the country of destination. However, the author is silent about the socio-political as well as security implications of the irregular migrants on the destination country.

The work of Francesco Castelli (2018), entitled *"Drivers of migration: why do people move?"* is praiseworthy as it nicely gives a theoretical orientation to the factors causing irregular migration. In this paper the author has mentioned about several factors driving irregular migration which can be brought under 'meso', 'micro' and 'macro factor'. Under the meso factor the author has brought communication technology, land grabbing and diasporic link, whereas under the micro factor education, religion, marital status and personal attitude to migrate have been included. Finally, under the macro factor the author has included the political, demographic, socio-economic and environmental situation. The author is of the opinion that all these factors play an important role in forcing the people to migrate to a foreign country. However, from this article no information can be collected regarding migration and security link in general.

In a paper entitled *"Pull and Push Factors of Migration: A Case Study in the Urban Area of Monywa Township, Myanmar"* Kyaing Kyaing, he describes about the migration pattern in Monywa which is a thriving capital city of North-West command and is located on the India, Myanmar and China trade route. In this article the author has followed the pull-push factors theory behind people migration to Monywa Township. However this article is limited to the study of migration in Monywa township and hence do not give a general picture of migration flow. Moreover this study is limited to the study of migration and lacks any information on migration-security linkage. In spite of this, the article gives sound understanding on the determinants of migration.

The European Asylum Support Office (2016) in a research project entitled *"Significant Pull/Push Factors for Determining of Asylum-Related Migration"* conducted review of various literatures which examines several factors influencing population movement form the country of origin to the country of destination within the European Union. It also examines the asylum claim of the migrants in the place of destination. The project analyses the people movement within the pull-push framework. However from this work, little is known about the security implications of international migration on the country of destination.

Umar Kari et. al. (2019), in their joint work entitled *"A Study of Illegal Migration Trends and the Pull and Push Factors in Nigeria, 2011–2017"*, starts with an explanation on the basic concept like irregular migration. The authors have also relayed on the pull-push determinants while highlighting about the reason behind trans-border migration. The paper recommends "that Industrialization of Africa, skill Acquisition and Human Capital Development will help mitigate the desire to illicitly migrate out of Nigeria". In this article the authors have done a commendable work in highlighting the Implications of illegal migration in Europe and Nigeria. At the final section of this paper, there have been some suggestions to solve the problem of illegal migration. How illegal migration has given birth to ruthless human trafficking and smuggling has been the main attraction in this paper. Thus this paper enriches our understanding on migration study with a focus on pull and push determinants of migration and its implications on the social, economic and security domain.

Hiranya K. Nath et. al. (2010), in their work entitled *"Illegal Migration into Assam: Magnitude, Causes, and Economic Consequences"*, describes about the diverse facets of unlawful movement into Assam from Bangladesh. In this paper, the authors are of the opinion that population pressure in Bangladesh has put pressure on the environment of the country. It has also derailed the life and livelihood opportunities of the people of the region and the population have subsequently forced to migrate to the native country India with the hope of getting better economic employment opportunities. In this article the authors have also described the beneficial outcome of migrants in the country of destination. At the same time the socio-political, economic and environmental impacts of irregular migrants in the destination country is another part of inquiry of this paper.

The works of Laura Chappell et. al. (2011), entitled "*The impacts of irregular migration*", is a nice endeavour as it gives a clear understanding on the impacts of irregular migration on the receiving place. In this work the authors have not only discussed about the negative consequences of irregular migration on the destination country but also describes about several plights of the migrants. They hold the view that, the migrants after their arrival in the destination country lack access to basic social protections, workers' rights, and are frequently the victims of exploitative practices. In this paper, the authors have also talked for the human settlement of the migrants in a foreign country.

Emma Aguila et. al. (2012), in their joint paper *"Migration's Effects on Origin and Destination Countries"* has discussed about the impact of migration on the wage structure of both the sending and receiving countries. However this paper is limited to the pattern of migration from Mexico to the United States and does not give general information from which inferences can be drawn.

R.K. Sinha (2018), in a paper entitled, *"Disastrous consequences of illegal immigrants"* clearly mentions about the negative impacts of irregular migrants on the socio-economic and political structures of India. He is of the opinion that the country India is facing problems like water shortage and there are also few jobs for hands. The infrastructure in the country is not well developed and there is increasing rate of population growth. So influx of irregular migrant population from the bordering countries like Bangladesh is adding to the ongoing problem. In a nutshell, this paper is a praiseworthy contribution as it gives a clear picture of the impacts of the irregular Bangladeshi migrants on the economy, culture and more importantly on the security of India. However the study of Sinha is limited to the India and Bangladesh.

Dilip Ratha (2010), in his wonderful work entitled *"Impact of Migration on Economic and Social Development: Review of Evidence and Emerging Issues"* describes about the developments impacts of migration on the economy and society of the country of origin and the receiving country. To him economic reason is the main determinant of international migration. He said that more than nine out of 10 international migrants move for economic reason rather than violent conflict, political persecution and trafficking. However, this generalisation may not be true to all the cases and hence generalisation cannot be done on this inference. An important thing to be noted here is, the author has clearly mention migration has positive economic impacts on the migrant households, the sending country as well as the receiving country. At the last section of this paper the author has given some recommendation for enhancing the positive economic impacts of migration for the development of a society.

Trishnashree Devi (2018), in a paper entitled *"Political Impact of Migration in Assam Politics"* has clearly narrated about the implications of Bangladeshi migrants on the demography, economy, socio-political framework and environment of Assam, a north-eastern state in India. Mainly this paper is an attempt to understand the political impacts of migration in Assam. How politicisation of the migration issue in Assam politics has made the issue more complicated is another area of inquiry in this paper. At the last section of this paper the author has given certain suggestions to bring out a peaceful solution to the problem. In a nutshell, this article is a praiseworthy contribution as it gives a lucid understanding on migration and security nexus in general and India in particular.

The Word Economic Forum (2017), in its outstanding work entitled *"Migration and its Impact on Cities"* focuses on the state of migration, internal and international, voluntary and involuntary. It also discusses about the various types of migration followed by an inquiry into the several causes of migration in the world today. Generally the migrants settle in various cities in the destination country after their arrival. So how those cities face the challenge of integration is the most important area of discussion in this paper. In fact, this paper is a very comprehensive work which touches several aspects of both internal and international migration in the present day world.

Karly Hurlock (2019), in her paper entitled *"Political and Economic Impacts of Irregular Migration across the Indo-Bangla Border"* describes the basic reason of illegal entry of people to the country of destination. She is of the opinion that the strict legal norms on movement between nations have pushed many individuals to choose illegal route to cross an international border. In the context of India, the author has clearly describes about the influx of migrants from the neighbouring country, Bangladesh. She said that, India's sound economic position, liberal democratic setup has been the main pull factors of Bangladeshi migration to the country. The issue of politicisation of migration issue by different political parties is another area of discussion in this article. Moreover, the negative impact of the migrants on the economy of India, mainly on its labour market has also been highlighted in this paper. Thus the author has done a nice work in highlighting the impacts which the irregular Bangladeshi migrants leave on the political and economic scenario of India.

## References

1. Brauch, Hans Gunter (2011) "Concepts of Security Threats, Challenges, Vulnerabilities and Risks" in H.G.; Oswald Spring, U.; Mesjasz, C.; Grin, J.; Kameri-Mobte, P.; Chourou, B.; Dunay, P.; Birkman, J. (eds.) *Coping with Global Environmental Change, Disasters, and Security Threats, Challenges, Vulnerabilities and Risks*, Berlin Heidelberg : Springer
2. "Traditional and non-traditional security issues in foreign policy," [Online: web] Accessed 7 March, 2019 URL: http://shodhganga.inflibnet.ac.in/bitstream/ 10603/29666/9/09_chapter%202.pdf
3. *ibid.*, p. 26.

4 . *ibid.*, p. 35.
5. *ibid.*, p. 36.
6. Anthony Mely Caballero, (2007) Non traditional Security and Multilateralism in Asia: Reshaping the Contours of Regional Security Architecture?, [Online: web] Accessed 28 November 2014 URL: http://www.stanleyfoundation.org/ publications/pab/pab07mely.pdf
7. Manwarning Max G. (2011), "The Strategic Logic of The Contemporary Security Dilemma" [Online: web] Accessed 6 May 2014 URL: http://www. globalsecurity.org/military/ library/report/2011/ssi_manwaring.pdf.
8. Maharana, Ashok. (2017), *Climate Change and Its Security Aspects: Threatening the Food Security of India, New Delhi:* Ruby Press and Co.
9. Kumar, Anand. (2011), *"Illegal Bangladeshi migration to India: Impact on internal security"* [Online: web] Accessed 20 February 2019, URL: https://doi.org/10.1080/09700161.2011.530988.
10. Panda, Architesh. (2010), "Climate-induced migration from Bangladesh to India: Issues and Challenges" [Online Web] Accessed 11 Sept. 2017 URL: file:///C:/Users/Dell/Downloads/SSRN-id2186397.pdf

# 2

## Irregular Migration-Threat to Peace and Security: A Theoretical Framework

Recently a great deal of emphasis has been placed to explore the link between irregular migration and the security of a country. It is now generally accepted that there exist a close relationship between irregular migration and the security of migrants receiving country. The external boundary of a state is also endangered due to illegal entry and settlement of outsiders. In the context of India many security analysts have already showed serious concern to the illegal entry of Bangladeshi migrants to India. Migration is a phenomenon which can be noticed since the beginning of the human civilisation. It is a process that is not only limited to the human beings, but it is also seen in the case of animals and birds who flees to other places in search of food or a safe habitat. Human civilisation has a long history of migration, both internal and external. In the earlier times it was a common phenomenon where people from one place, having their distinct culture and language, were fleeing to another place in search of a better habitation. However, it is only in the recent decades, concerns have been shown among the scholars, academicians and various institutions to study the migration trend, its causes and impacts. The world after cold war is marked by many developments in international environment where scholars, academicians and also various institutions both at national, regional and international level have explored a new world having its new issues, challenges and concerns. Among the contemporary issues and challenges irregular migration from outside of the external boundary of a state has become a matter of worries for many countries. Even it has been considered as threat or challenge to peace and security of many host countries. Irregular migration from Mexico to America and from Bangladesh to India can be a case in point. Thus the central point of inquiry in this section is to explore the irregular migration and its security linkage in general.

## Basic Concepts on International Migration and Security

### Migration:

Before having an understanding regarding the concept of irregular migration it is desirable to know and understand the exact meaning of migration. In common perception, migration can be understood as the movement of people from one place to another. The International Organisation for Migration (IOM) defines Migration as "The movement of a person or a group of persons, either across an international border, or within a State. It is a population movement, encompassing any kind of movement of people, whatever its length, composition and causes; it includes migration of refugees, displaced persons, economic migrants, and persons moving for other purposes, including family reunification". It is to be noted that while the majority of migrants leave their native place in search of work and economic and social opportunities, a relatively small percentage of migrants are people who leave their country due to armed conflict, natural disaster, famine or persecution. The United Nations "reports that the number of international migrants worldwide reached 232 million in 2013, up from 175 million in 2000 and 154 million in 1990"[1].

### Irregular Migrants:

There exist a great deal of uncertainty regarding the terminologies i.e. irregular migrant, illegal migrant, undocumented migrant or clandestine migrant. These are some terms which are used interchangeably by scholars. However all these terms do not reflect the same meaning. Among the above mentioned terms the use of irregular is preferable to illegal migrants, because the latter caries criminal connotation and is seen denying migrants their humanity status. Credit goes to the United Nations in devising term like irregular migration keeping in view the human rights of all the displaced people who crosses an international border due to certain compulsions in their own country. This concept had its origin in the United Nations General Assembly Resolution on measures to ensure the human rights and dignity of all migrant workers (9th December 1975). The General Assembly requests the United Nations Organs and specialised agencies concerned to utilise in all official documents the term "non documented or irregular migrant workers to define those workers that illegally enter another country to obtain work". Moreover the European Union (EU) Parliamentary Assembly issued Resolution 1509 (2006) Human Rights of Irregular Migration (27 June 2006), which states in Article-7 that Assembly prefers to use the term 'irregular migrants' to other terms such as 'illegal migrants' or 'migrants without papers'. The European Union also asks its institutions and member states to stop using the term illegal migrants, because of its negative connotation. It rather prefers irregular/undocumented migrants to illegal migrants. Therefore the most preferable term, irregular migrant is used because it gives importance to human rights of the migrants; otherwise it would result in their alienation, marginalisation, discrimination and violence[2].

According to the International Organisation for Migration (IOM) "an irregular migrant is a person who, owing to unauthorised entry, breach of condition of entry, or expiry of his or her visa, lacks legal status in a transit or host country". Irregular migration, therefore, refers to "Movement takes place outside the regulatory norms of the sending, transit and receiving countries.... From the perspective of destination countries it is entry, stay or work in a country without the necessary authorisation or documents required under immigration regulations. From the perspective of the sending country, the irregularity is, for example, seen in cases in which a person crosses an international boundary without a valid passport or travel document or does not fulfil the administrative requirements for leaving the country" (International Organisation for Migration, 2011). Moreover "Irregular migration includes a variety of movements and status that conflicts with migration laws in both migrant-transit and migrant-receiving countries and taken its broadest definition, encompasses illegal entry, overstaying visas, remaining as a rejected asylum-seeker and engaging in prohibited" [3] work. There are three grounds on the basis of which the use of the term 'illegal' can be criticised. First, the term illegal is always associated with criminality. All the irregular migrants cannot be criminals. The UN Special Reporteur on the Rights of Non-citizens, in its final report recommends that: "Immigrants... even those who are in a country illegally and whose claims are not considered valid by the authorities, should not be treated as criminals". Second, if we define a person as illegal then it will undermine his humanity and dignity. It can simply be forgotten that such migrants are human beings who possess fundamental rights whatever their status is. "Third, and of the particular concern to the Office of the United Nations High Commissioner on Refugees (UNHCR) is the possibility that labelling as illegal asylum seekers who find themselves in an irregular situation may further jeopardise their asylum claims"[4].

**New Concept of Security:**

In military and strategic point, security is defined as the nonexistence of military clash. However today many scholars are not in support of such conception and they take it as narrowly defined. They are of the opinion that the concept of security should be broadly analysed as it includes a wide range of issues. As there are more threats and dangers which need to be considered today, it is not sufficient to articulate of security as merely nonexistence of military clash in political science discourse. A huge number of threat or dangers have appeared today. Environmental catastrophe, international or global terrorism, fatal infections and diseases, starvation, criminal fighting and economic or financial exploitation are few examples of these threats and all these should be taken into consideration while defining the concept of security.

Security has mainly two basic dimensions, one is objective and other is subjective security. The objective dimension of security relays on the fact of being protected from danger, where as the subjective security is the genuine feeling of safety. However, the concept of security does not revolve round on a general precise definition, it deals with a wide range of danger, and possibility that is too much to grasp. Considering all these things it can be said that security is the search of freedom from any threat but a wide-ranging and clear-cut definition is hard to reach[5].

**The Process of Securitisation:**

In order to understand the process of and the need of securitisation of irregular migration, it is pertinent to know exactly the meaning and the process of securitisation. In this sphere securitisation refers to how social issues are constructed into issue of security. In other words, securitisation is the process where a social issue is constructed into a security issue. According to Barry Buzan, when a problem is presented to an existential danger to the referent then we talk about security. Here the referent is the object that needs to be protected. Thus in the securitisation process non-politicised issue becomes politicised and finally become a security issue. Moreover the securitisation process contains three components namely the securitising act, a securitising actor and an audience[6].

The securitising act is the rhetorical act of using terms of security in relations to certain events and development. In this sphere the issue is discursively emphasised as a threat or danger. The securitising actor refers to the actor who attempts to securitize an issue and who is in a position of authority and commands political legitimacy in order to be able to convince the audience about the threat. Thus the securitising actor and institutions need some sort of credibility in the eyes of the audience. The "audience is the consumer of the speech act who has the ability to enable the securitising actor" [7] to act in a particular way.

## Irregular Migration: The Idea of its Securitisation

The world after cold war is marked by many international developments in international politics. It not only brought an end to the decades long nerve war under the political leadership of the United States of America and the Soviet Union of Russia, but also ushered an era of a new world order where one can notice many changes in social, economic, political and security domain of the countries of the world. Globalisation became an unavoidable reality which brought all the nations of the world under a global village. There took place many developments in science, art, technology, and transportation and communication system. The possession of nuclear weapons by all most all the nations of the world has become a reality now. Along with the changing scenario of international environment there also took place significant changes in the security concern for nation states. The scholars, researchers and many government and non-government organisations showed a renewed concern to the security of a country. This is in the sense that, in this time military threat perception lost its importance. War, aggression, or military attacks are no longer considered to be security threats today, as it was considered before the end of the cold war. The effective functioning of various international and regional organisations at the world level has limited the possibility of a military attack by a state. Again, the possession of nuclear weapons and its catastrophic consequences seen in Japan (in 1945) has created a major deterrence which minimises the chances of conflict reaching to the state of confrontation and war among Nations. Thus the massive changes in the security domain as a whole necessitated the task of redefining the prevailing notion of security threat. The threat perception has become fundamentally changed now and the concept of security has undergone a big transformation. Today the world focuses on many challenges to its security that may endanger its very existence. Climate change and global warming, international terrorism, drug trafficking, energy shortage, cross-border irregular migration, emergence of deadly diseases and many others have been included under the security discourses now as all these poses serious threat to the security of the world.

## The Process of Securitisation of Migration

In the recent decades many countries of the world are experiencing a rise in international migration. The concept of securitisation was first included under the security studies by the Copenhagen School of Security Studies. Barry Buzan, Ole Waever and Jaap de Wilde of the Copenhagen School started giving a new notion to the concept of security in the post cold war era. The Copenhagen School suggests that the state is not the single referent object for which security will be sought. A book entitled 'Security: A New Framework for Analysis' talks for expansion of the subject of security which will include not merely the military sector, but five categories: military, economic, environmental, societal and political[8].

Keeping in view the above realities in mind, migration is an issue which need to be securitised today for the interest of mankind because there exist a close link between security of a Nation and irregular migration. "The process in which migration discourse shift towards an emphasis on security has been referred to as the securitisation of migration"[9]. International migration, particularly irregular inflow of population has become a key security issue and is perceived in some eyes as existential security threat. Scholars have referred to the current state of affairs as securitised migration or as the securitisation of migration. In other words, when an issue is securitised then certain measures are taken to neutralise the bad effects of that problem. For example, when irregular migration is securitised then the affected countries adopt more restrictive migration and asylum policies, new surveillance and control devices and tighter external border controls. Thus it is due to this probable threat such measures are taken and justified. Irregular migration is securitised due to two main reasons. Firstly, migration has the potentiality to cause future crisis in a society due to large scale inflow of migrants. Secondly, due to its connection with criminal activity it is brought under security discourse. In securitising migration the referent object need to be protected from the imminent threat. From the economic point of view migration possess the potentially to destabilise the economy by over burdening the economic condition. Another referent object in the securitising process of migration is the language, culture and tradition of the community. It is true that migration is an unsafe action for the people concerned, at the same time it is also essential to think of the migrants as they are also victims of many dangers. Thus the migrants are also referent objects in the process of securitisation. Migrants are said to be the victim of cross-border crimes like human trafficking, abuse and exploitation, particularly in the border and in the labour market of the destination country. Therefore human rights are the central part of migration policy and in the process of securitisation of migration[10].

In a nutshell, two different referent objects are constructed in the securitisation process of migration i.e. first the people of the destination and second the migrants themselves. It is not that only the people, economy and other factors of the destination country are seen as being exposed to threat, but the migrants are also seen as victims as they are exposed to dangerous situation. Thus in devising policy framework there is necessity to properly protect the human rights of the migrants without ignoring the fact that irregular migration is a serious security threat and hence needs to be regulated.

## Migration and Future Crisis

Migration is in common perception seen as a flow which constructs a picture of migrants as a power or a phenomenon, not as individuals. Thus the term flow has a threatening connotation which talks about migration control and its management to avert any future crisis. The state becomes overburdened to handle where the number of migrants is higher. The threat perception is also higher in such a situation. So the state takes resort to various measures and instruments for managing the crisis. Thus it finally creates the picture of a potential risk caused by huge migration flows[11].

### Migration and Criminal Activity:

Mostly, the irregular migrants are seen with suspicion and are thought to be linked with many criminal activities. However, refugees or legal migrants are not so connected with crimes. Refugees are themselves sufferers and are in need of the security. Whereas officially permitted migrants are treated as economic prospect. But some of the irregular migrants are associated with unlawful activity and hence not required in the destination. Thus there emerges the voice to fight or combat irregular migration.

These crimes are often explained as cross border offence and are frequently done by organised criminal faction and are threat to the internal security. Thus there is need to securitize irregular migration. The European Union declared that, "A broad understanding of security means that irregular migration also needs to be considered in connection with organised crimes and lack of rule of law and justice, feeding on corruption and inadequate regulation".

Terrorism and violent fanaticism is also connected with

irregular migration. Many cases highlights that people are recruited trained and are sent to other country to become a freedom fighter in that country, to which we call terrorist. Thus in one of the European Union document, it has been commonly articulated that "Over the past years several terrorist attacks have been taken place, mostly by individuals or smaller groups but many with severe consequences. The threat from terrorism and violent extremism will pose a serious challenge to EU in the coming years. There is worrying trend with mostly young people going to other countries such as Syria to foreign fighter".

To summarise, there are two ways in which irregular migration can be securitised. The first way is to connect migration with future crisis or emergency caused by massive migrant inflows, which is considered as a threat. The second is to connect irregular migration with criminal activities which threatens both internal and external security and hence there is need of securitising irregular migration. At the same time the fundamental human rights of the migrants need to be considered in the securitisation process.

**Emergence of Irregular Migration as a Security Threat in the United States:**

Since its creation, the United States of America has been treated as an attractive destination for the migrants and the issue of migration was never considered to be a threat to the security of the US earlier. However after September 11, 2001 terrorist attack on its soil, the country became alert and the concept of migration as a security threat was emerged. Since then migration was not considered as common social issue having its impacts on jobs and welfare facilities but it was seriously viewed as a security issue. The book entitled 'Immigration and Security: Post-9/11 in the United States' written by John Tirman which was published in 2006, illustrates changes in the understanding of migration after 9/11 terrorist attack. Thus after 9/11 attack, terrorism was kept in central focus while developing any discourse or policies on migration. The migrants from Arab, Latin America and Mexico were affected after that. Moreover a number of politicians and intellectuals raised the issue of migration from Mexico as a security threat to the America[12].

**Surfacing of Migration as Security Issue in European Union:**

In contrast to the United States of America the issue of terrorism was not the driving factor to securitize migration. Even after the 9/11 attack on the America the issue of migration was not considered as a security issue in the European Union. Protection of the European Identity and culture encouraged by the idea of "Fortress Europe" was the major motivating factor for securitising migration in the EU. The conception of "Fortress Europe" is founded on two things i.e. free mobility and the elimination of internal borders, focusing on exclusive border management. Also the arguments that the migrants possess the potentiality to threaten the EU's economy created ground for development of more restrictive migration policy. It also paved the way for framing migration as a security issue. Huysman a well known scholar illustrates this phenomenon as conversion of an "economic project of the internal market into an internal security project"[13].

## Determinants of Irregular Migration

It is not easy to point out the exact and specific reasons which force people or group to leave their own country in search of a new one. A number of interlinked factors are responsible in this connection which forces a person to migrate voluntarily or otherwise. Unwanted situation in their home state which is unbearable and intolerable creates personal whims and consequently compel them to search for a safe haven. Many compulsions such as social, political, economic or even environmental factors back in their home country can be acted as push factors behind a person who leave his homeland and inhabit in a new nation. There are also certain pull factors such as accessibility of land, healthier financial opportunities or employment, better education, health services and similar culture which attracts these migrants to that place. For the purpose of better understanding, the push factors behind migration can be categorised into the following four categories such as, socio-political, economic, environmental and other facilitating factors.

**Socio-Political Factors:**

It is one of the major reasons among the push factors, which forces many people to leave their home country and to search for a new place crossing an international border. In many poor and backward countries the socio-political conditions make it completely impossible for the affected people to stay there and hence force them to migrate either temporarily or permanently. Communal riots, hatred and intolerance are certain political factors having disastrous impacts upon the life of the people which have always been criticised because of its destabilising impacts upon the common life. In communal riots the atrocities against specific community forces the vulnerable group to search for such place where there life could be safe and secure. They particularly migrate to such areas where they have pre-religious and cultural link. The communal riots of 1950s and 1960s in East Bengal (now Bangladesh) can be the best illustration of this fact. These migrants, however, makes a permanent settlement in the receiving country having no intention to go back to their home state. In the course of time they try to obtain land, voter identity card and most of them even successful in their endeavour. In a nutshell communal riots coupled with state's indifferences towards their plights and the discriminatory attitudes are the basic political factors behind migration.

In fact, there are certain regions or country where the government is not secular and shows favourable attention to a particular religious community; it becomes very pathetic for other section of people (the religious minorities) to sustain there. The discriminatory policies on land, house, income etc, create many hazardous for them and when they try to resent they faces the torture inflicted by the state. Thus state's atrocities and indifferences is to a great extent compels the victims to leave their own country and cross an international border. In a religious based state, as the head of the government adopts discriminatory policies, which support only a particular religious group, it becomes very difficult and miserable for another community to live there.

**Economic Factors:**

Apart from the socio-political reasons which are mainly responsible for driving a section of people out of their home country, a number of economic factors are also responsible for mass migration from one country to another. In the case of a communal clashes or any government's apathy to the problem of a section of people, a particular group of people are affected which forces them to migrate. However, economic reason crosses this communal or religious boundary and a weak economic condition can force people, irrespective of their religious or community linkage, to migrate crossing an international border. For example, due to numerous economic reasons back in their home, millions of Bangladeshi nationals, both Hindu and Muslim, have been forced to abandon their home country and have entered India illegally.

Among the economic reasons, land alienation along with poor of employment opportunities are major causes compelling a vast section of affected people to migrate internationally. Government's discriminatory policies, in some cases, are responsible for people's weak economic condition which disposes a huge number of people of their familial property. Besides this, pressure of increasing population on scarce resources, environmental disaster resulting in devastation of agriculture, fisheries etc are also equally responsible for mass migration. "Growing population creates greater demands on resources such as land, food, energy, water and forest products, and their consequent overuse results in deterioration of quality. This process in turn, encourages inequality in resources distribution among the rich and poor as the rich corner them and deny the poor their share. The shifting of resources in the favour of the rich pushes the poor to greater misery triggering out migration"[14].

In a country, where agriculture or other related sectors are key source of livelihood of a major section of people, any deviation in the agricultural output will directly put pressure on the quality of life of the people. Moreover, increasing population in a country will also force the farmers to produce more and more, and this consequently result in the use of chemicals and other means for more production. However, this practice is not sustainable as it reduces soil quality and put pressure on agricultural land. It deprives the soil from important organic matter and consequently leads to land degradation and low production. Due to all these problems people are frustrated with the agricultural work and search for other option to earn their livelihood. In such situation they migrate either to urban areas or even chose for international migration when the urban setup is insufficient to adjust them and to fulfil their basic needs.

Lacks of adequate job opportunities are also responsible for large scale migration. In a country where agricultural sector is unable to provide sufficient job then people opt for industrial work where they are appointed as industrial labourer. Industrialisation is to a great extent, vital for a nation as it helps in poverty alleviation. It employs a large section of people in the industrial activities and also contributes to the GDP of a country. However, in all those countries where industrialisation has not been able to give employment opportunities to its growing labour force, it gives birth to high rate of unemployment. Thus the working class people, being unable to get a suitable job in their home state, decide to go outside for better employment[15].

In underdeveloped or backward countries, where the government does not have any employment generation schemes for its labour forces, the people decide to move to another country for better job avenues. Thus, even without a labour demand in the receiving country there takes place the movement of people who cross over another country clandestinely. Many scholars have argued that irregular migration is a self-rescue migration where the migrants choose to leave their home country due to "poverty, hunger, political and religious persecution, governmental apathy" and so on, than response to demand for labour forces in the receiving country[16].

**Environmental Factors:**

Harsh environmental impact upon the life of the people is a major factor results in out migration of people who crosses an international border. Environmental hazards, due to rapid changes in the climate condition of the Earth, weaken a state's economic and political strength. Devastating effects of climate change on agriculture derails the very existence of an overwhelming number of people who are dependent upon agriculture or related sectors. It attacks on the source of livelihood of people and push them to abysmal poverty. It is not possible for poor farmers with small land holding to sustain their family throughout the year. And such a condition becomes more complicated due to climate hazards like floods and droughts which consequently results in famine forcing the affected people to migrate.

Thus environmental change can increase the rate of migration. Environmental change in the form of floods, droughts, cyclones, heat and cold waves are intensified and can cause serious lose to the agriculture and economy of the people. It can also seriously affect the life of all those people who are indirectly dependent upon agriculture to earn their livelihood.

Short term and long term migration can take place due to draught. Finding no other option, people chose to migration route as an adaptive strategy during the drought period. Historically it has been observed that drought has caused permanent migration of people. "Benson Peterson and Stein suggest that severe droughts in the 12$^{th}$ and 13$^{th}$ centuries may have impacted migration and abandonment of a number of pre-Columbian Native American villages"[17].

Soil degradation and unsustainable agricultural practices are also linked to out migration of people. It has been observed that, migration has been used as a survival strategy. It is to be noted that, environmental factor alone does not lead to migration, a number of other drivers are also important here which plays a vital role behind a person's decision to migrate.

Flooding, which is the result of extreme climate event, is also a major push factor of migration. After Cyclone Alia, there took place huge migration of people who belonged to lower socio-economic segments of Bangladesh society. And people opted for the migration route because of the necessity to diversify their income. The helplessness to restore their broken property also forced them to migrate. However, in developed countries the rate of migration due to flooding is very low. This is because of the public efforts at disaster mitigation, and protection in the flood prone areas. The government's support also reduces the chance of migration of people as is seen in United States[18].

In a nutshell, environmental stress upon the life and livelihood of a large section people, who are dependent upon climate sensitive ecosystem for earning their livelihood, can be a major push factor behind mass migration. When the socio-economic condition of people are broken, and the government shows its inability to repair them to bring normalcy in the life of its people, then people are forced to abandon their home country and are migrated to all those region where they will have a chance to survive at least. For example, the geographical location of Bangladesh has made it vulnerable to many environmental hazards like floods, cyclones etc., and when people's livelihood are seriously damaged due to natural calamities they are forced to migrate to urban areas with a hope to get a source to earn their livelihood. However, the densely populated urban area, insufficient to adjust the people, compels them for out migration crossing an international border.

**Other Facilitating Factors:**

It is not so easy for an individual to leave his or her home, family and dear ones in search of a better life in another country. Situation forces them to take such an extreme step even at the risk of their life. The unsafe political, religious, social and economic situation back in their own countries leaves them helpless with no other option except migration with the hope of finding a safe place. In all those countries, where there is no peace and security, persecution, tribal conflicts, political turmoil and socio-economic problems are very pronounced, the rate of migration is very high[19]. Moreover gender, age, apprehension of impending disaster and "calamity in the home state, availability and accessibility of land, adequate employment opportunities, and a sense of safety and security in intended area of migration along with family and kinship" [20] network shapes migration decision.

No doubt, due to many unbearable and unavoidable situation people are forced to take migration decision, but there are certain factors which gives force and strengthen people's decisions to migrate crossing an international border. The pre-cultural and linguistic ties with the people of the receiving country can be facilitating factor in this connection. And the case of Bangladeshi migrants in India can be case in point. If the border between migrants sending and migrants receiving countries is porous, then also it makes their entry to the receiving country easier.

In the case of similarity in the ethnic composition of the migrant people and the local inhabitants in the destination it becomes difficult to differentiate between migrants and the citizens. Moreover the old migrants in the receiving country provides help to the new migrants starting from their clandestine movement to the obtaining of job and land in the receiving country.

Other important facilitating factors, often causes out-migration is the political patronage given to the illegal migrants in the receiving country. This has always been a helping aspect encouraging millions of migrants to settle in a foreign country. The politics of vote bank has always influenced the political parties to give citizen status to the migrants in that country. No doubt there have been many demands or even struggle to detect and deport the migrants who are settled illegally, but all the attempts have been crumbled under political pressures.

When the security forces guarding the borders are in connection with the migrant smugglers, who play a vital role in the clandestine entry of the migrants, then it becomes very easy to enter the country without proper documents. Thus all the above mentioned factors have facilitated smooth migration from one country to another.

## Pull Factors of Irregular Migration

Besides the factors that compel the people to leave their own country, there are also certain factors that attract the affected people to the country and these can be termed as pull factors behind mass migration. For the purpose of better understanding, these factors can be categorised under the following headings.

Migration decision is not the first choice of the people who are migrated. Various compulsions that can be unavoidable force them to migrate. At the same time people's decision to migrate is also associated with some factors that attract them to a destination country. And these attracting factors can be brought under the category of pull factors. In short, to migrate, people view their current place of residence so negatively that they feel pushed away, and they view another place so attractive that they feel pulled towards it. Thus the positive aspects attract them to that country.

**Economic Factor:**

In contrast to the pathetic condition of life and the poor wages, when the people see a better quality of life and better economic opportunities coupled with high wages, they decides to migrate even to a foreign country. In other words, economic incentives act as potential pull factor for migration decision. When high wages is given in abroad in comparison to the very low wages in their home country, then people move to that country with the intention to get rid of their poor condition. In addition to this, the social welfare measures undertaken in the destination country also assures them of a good quality of life even in case they are unable to work.

Another thing to be noted here is that, unemployment in their home country does not merely act as a push factor for migration. The disparity of the wages given to the workers can be a major determinant of migration decision. The rate of unemployment may be low in the sending country; however the huge wage rate attracts people to that country. For example, in America, the Mexican migrants coming to the former do not merely leave their home country due to unemployment at home. In fact, in recent years the rate of unemployment in Mexico has remained significantly lower than the US[21].

Labour demands in a country can also attract many people to migrate. The increasing demands of skilled workers generally provide greater employment opportunities with wage which is more satisfying in comparison to their own country and hence the consequence is the migration inflow to the place of destination. There are millions of job that the domestic workers may refuse to fill because of their low wages and minimal opportunities in professional advancement. The case of Canada can be the best example here, where the country's migrant population has nearly doubled over the past couple of years[22].

Thus certain theories on migration assumes individual as rational utility-maximising agents who opt for migration decision for a better standard of living. The difference in wage and living standard between people of the origin and destination country shapes human mobility, both internal and international. And this migration can take place either through licit or illicit means[23]. However Czaika and de Hass are of the opinion that poverty and economic hardship of an individual may act as an intervening factors limiting people's ability to migrate even if they are aware of the expected higher earnings in the destination country[24].

The development in the information and communication technologies in the modern times familiarised about the living condition of the destination country to the people of the sending country. So this knowledge on the living standard of the people of the destination country shapes their aspiration to migrate.

Again, the presence of the family and the friend networks in the destination country can be a pull factor and can cause migration movement. It also influences people's preferences for the destination country. Cummings et al, says that "irregular migration is, in most cases, the result of a collective effort made by families in which family, social and religious networks, increasingly facilitated by the use of social media, play a crucial role in deciding the timing and circumstances of individual movement"[25].

"On the macro level, migration scholar also generally confirmed that human mobility is shaped by the inherent characteristics of global capitalist expansion– namely the structural demand for cheap and exploitable labour in industrialised countries– coupled with social dynamics (e.g. limited native labour supply or unwillingness of the native workers to take on low-paid, unstable jobs)"[26].

An important factor shaping migration movement need to be analysed as it causes migration of the people mostly through irregular channels. Labour demand in sectors like domestic care, attracts more female workers. Many scholars have opined that constant labour requirement in receiving countries, along with labour migration schemes or migration policies causes in irregular migration[27].

In a nutshell the economic pull factor behind migration decision can be analysed keeping in view certain factors i.e. high living standard, high wages, advancement in communication technologies, the unwillingness of the people of the destination country to work in certain sectors etc. Thus people's decision to migrate is not shaped by a single economic factors, rather multiple of factors work in this spheres.

**Political and Security Factor:**

When discrimination, persecution, political instability, civil war or human trafficking acts as strong push factors for the affected people to leave their home country, then the existence and working of a tolerant government, that implements democratic principles as opposed to authoritarian rule, can be pull factors attracting many people to that country. In other words the operation of a liberal democratic government, constantly working for the welfare of its people with secularism as it centre, can make the country more attractive to the potential migrants. In the transitional societies affected with constant civil unrest, people find it difficult to survive. There also exists the frequent danger of human trafficking. Such a disturbed society creates favourable environment for organised crimes, including trafficking in persons. Thus, the vulnerable people see a ray of hope to survive in those countries where there exist respect to humanity and human rights. The people's centric nation with a democratic setup always attracts those people who are fleeing from gross human rights violation[28]. "Political conditions can also operate as pull factors. People may be attracted to democratic countries that encourage individual choice in education, career, and place of residence. After Communists gained control of Eastern Europe in the late 1940s, many people in that region were pulled toward the democracies in Western Europe and North America. Communist governments in Eastern Europe clamped down on emigration for fear of losing their most able workers. The most dramatic symbol of restricted emigration was the Berlin Wall, which the Communists built to prevent emigration from Communist-controlled East Berlin into democratic West Berlin"[29].

Thus in the forced and irregular migration literature political or security factors emerges as a significant determinant of migration. Insecurity and political crisis could challenge the survival of the people and consequently forces them to migrate. In fact, a country, which is free from internal conflict, harassment, discrimination and torture of people who disagree with government, can be an attractive place for those people who suffer from all these human predicaments. Equal treatment to all the religious belief and faith, freedom of religion as granted by the Constitution of country can also attract people who are handicapped by a theocratic society.

**Past-Historical, Cultural and Geographical Ties:**

Past historical ties, linguistic similarities and geographical distance can significantly act as major determinant of migration. When the people of the sending country find similar language, culture or any pre-linkage with the destination country then decide to migrate in the case of any such need. This is because similar culture, language or other similarities can help them to mix with the people of the destination country and there is very few chance of being identified as migrant and deportation. Again, if the geographical distance between the migrant origin and migrant destination country is small then it can lead to migration movement significantly[30]. The case between India and Bangladesh can be a better illustration in this context.

Grogger and Hanson in their study held the view that similarities in language spoken among the people of origin and destination country appears as a major factor in causing bilateral migration flow[31].

**Environmental Factor:**

Environmental factor can be both pull and push factor behind migration decision of people. Climate change and the resultant environmental hazards breakdown the backbone of those people who are dependent upon climate sensitive ecosystem for their livelihood. These people, finding no other suitable option, are pulled towards geographically attractive regions where the amount of climate hazards is relatively low. Generally an attractive climate for migrants includes river basin and a stable warm climate. A warm winter climate attracts many migrants to its region. People are also pulled towards that climate zone where they can invest in agriculture and related sectors with the assurance of getting maximum output.

As availability of water can better contribute to the agriculture and other house hold activities, people decides to migrate to all those areas where there is substantive water. Generally river basins are more attractive for farming and fisheries. Again, all those areas which are not affected with environmental hazards like drought, flood and cyclone attract many people who are suffered by all these natural disasters. Bangladesh's geographical location has made its people vulnerable to frequent droughts and floods and hence forcing the people to search for a safe haven where these environmental problems will be less. Thus the places free from environmental hazards like flooding, earthquakes, tsunami and hurricanes attract a lot of people to its region.

**Better Health and Education Facilities:**

Many scholars are of the opinion that better health care facilities and educational opportunities can attract many people to migrate legally or illicitly. In the backward and underdeveloped countries the infrastructure are not fully developed and hence are unable to provide its population a better health care system. Thus many hazardous and infectious diseases appear in an uncontrolled way taking the life of many people. Moreover, the changing climate condition and the process of globalisation have given birth to severe health epidemics which have become a serious challenge for the country to tackle.

Again, the high cost for better medical treatment coupled with undeveloped medical sector have forced many people to settle in all those places where they can get better health care facilities in an affordable cost. In a nut shell, better health care system along with government's initiatives and activeness to tackle many health hazards can be an attractive factor for the affected people. Moreover, educational development and affordable price for education can always be a major determinant attracting many migrant students.

## Changes in the Destination Country due to Irregular Migration

In all those countries where the population growth is already high, an extra burden of population due to migration is certainly a big problem. These countries witness many changes in its social, political and economic spheres due to migration influx. Increasing number of population put pressure upon the already stretched resources like water, land, forest etc. Water scarcity becomes a big problem in such areas. Occupation of land by the migrants makes the destination overcrowded which in turn causes problem in transportation, and communication. Thus irregular migration flow add problem to the country which are already in stress.

As the migrants are ready to work in low prices they change the wage structure in the destination country. Again they also take away the jobs from the hands of the locals. Migrants clear the forest, occupy the government land, make the place overcrowded and finally pollute the environment and biodiversity. It has also been noticed that the terrorist network recruits from the migrants and uses them against the destination country. In this way there takes place the infiltration of terrorists. Moreover, excessive population influx changes the local cultural pattern and a sense of identity crisis begin among the locals. Thus the irregular migration causes multiple of challenges in the country of destination.

All these impacts on the social, economic, political and environmental spheres can be discussed as below:

**Social Sphere:**

Many discourses on migration focus on the social impacts of irregular migration on the destination country. These impacts are studied in the context of crime and security because some irregular migrants do get involved in serious criminal network due to many compulsions. After 9/11 terrorist attack, irregular migration has been securitised and there are also many evidences that the terrorist network use the irregular migrants to further their aims. It is also true that the migrants themselves feel threatened by terrorist activity.

***Threat to the Local Identity:***

Migration influx basically causes identity crisis in the destination country. Among the indigenous people a sense of threat regarding the loss of their own identity begin to emerge. As they feel overwhelmed by the migration flow, they see their cultural survival in jeopardy, their political control is in weaken position and also their employment opportunity is also undermined by the migrants. And this feeling is because of the fact that the migrants are failed to identify with the mainstream of the society. Thus it leads to a sense of insecurity among the local people and the consequence can be seen in the form of many group violence and conflict[32].

*Environmental Stress:*

Environmental degradation in the form of land encroachment by the migrants can be a major consequence on the society of the destination country. After their arrival there takes place encroachment of large areas of forest land by the migrants. They convert that land into their places for settlement and cultivation. Thus there takes place serious decline in the percent of land areas. As the forest is declined, it leaves negative impacts upon the ecosystem and the biodiversity. Also it makes the area over crowded and polluted[33].

When a place is overcrowded due to migration influx, it leads to serious community tension and it also becomes difficult for the police to control such a situation. "The Commission on Integration and Cohesion found that tension usually exist with the presence of high level of migration combined with other form of social exclusion like poverty, poor housing etc"[34].

**Economic Sphere:**

*Stress on Government:*

In a democratic country the government is responsible for the welfare of its people. It provides them various facilities in the spheres of health, education, housing, road, transportation, communication etc. The government has to spend enormous amount of money to provide all these facilities to its entire people. However, the migration influx in the destination country increases state's expenditure as the government has to bear extra- burden for the migrants. Thus, it seriously increases "pressure on the part of the government as the government has to increase the expenditure on education"[35], health, and other facilities for the migrants.

*Competition over Job:*

Competition over the job between the migrants and the local people is a serious economic consequence due to irregular entry of foreigners. There is a fear that the migrants will displace the local workers from their job. It is also a fact that the migrants are ready to work even in low prices. Moreover, they are ready to work in all those sectors where the local people may deny. Thus there is a fear, particularly during recession that migrants take jobs which would otherwise be taken by the local people. Competition over job obliviously leads to conflict and law and order problem.

***Deterioration of the Labour Market:***

Along with changes in political landscape of the destination country, the irregular migrants also change the labour market. They negatively impact the labour market of the destination country by increasing competition over jobs, particularly in the informal sector where the majority of the migrants will find employment. This changes the wage structures as they are ready to work with low prices. Consequently unemployed local workers will be less likely to find employment and even those who do find employment will face lower wages. These "wage-depressing effects of irregular migration results in decreased consumption and investment on the part of the workers, effectively decreasing capital accumulation for the host" [36]country.

**Political Sphere:**

***Law and Order Problem:***

People resentment to the irregular migrants can be a harsh reality when these migrants seriously influence the economy, society and environment of the destination country. Overcrowding, competition over job, threat to local language, culture and tradition are the obvious outcome. This gives rise to conflict and agitation by the local people. Moreover, the failure of the existing government to tackle the issue of migration results in serious law and order problem. And such problem consequently takes the form of violence which causes instability, ethnic violence and internal disturbances[37].

### *Disturb the Election Process:*

Irregular population migration also disturbs the election process in the receiving country. Mainly some political party shows favour to them in the hope of enriching their vote bank. Many migrants are also successful in obtaining voter identity card and exercise the right to vote. Thus they claim to be a citizen in a destination country. Thus many fake voters or foreign citizen enter the political arena and influence the voting process.

In some cases it has been noticed that some political parties are very much interested to give the migrants the status of citizen only to enrich their vote bank. Thus they welcome the migrants to maintain their political viability. The political leaders promise the migrants of providing security and other facilities in return of voting in their favour. In this way the foreigners get the right to vote in a destination country which necessarily disturbs the true democratic election process[38].

### *Conflict over Language:*

Migrants are those people who come to the destination with their own language and scripts. Excessive population influx changes the demographic structure of the destination along with local culture and language. When the locals are reduced to a minority, they may lose their own language as the government of the concerned place may give recognition to the language of the migrants due to vote bank politics. Assam, a North-East state of India, can be the best example of it.

### *Politics of Communalism:*

The political landscape of the destination country witness and experience political communalism due to political patronage granted to the irregular migrants. In some cases the political parties start communal politics and follow the policy of appeasement to gain electoral victory. Thus it seriously upset the local people[39].

Thus the destination country witness many changes in its social, economic, political and environmental set up due to population influx into it. Although migration inflow have some positive impacts for the destination country as it makes available labour forces, also contributes to the GDP of the country, however its negative impacts overweight its few positive impacts. Moreover, in those countries where the infrastructure is not fully developed coupled with an existing high population, an extra population movement generally creates challenges for the country to accommodate with such a situation. In other words it creates the challenge of integration for the destination country. Whatever may be the fact associated with irregular migration, there have been consensus among many scholars, policymakers, and researchers to securitize irregular migration due to its destabilising effects on the people of the country of destination.

## Irregular Migration: Its Impact on Various Dimensions of National Security

The national security of a country can be defined as the freedom from threat which endangers the existence and progress of a society and state. Major elements of national security are state's capability and self-sufficiency, balance of power and the safety and security of its people and institutions. And all these elements are adversely affected by illegal migration flow. Excessive influx of population in a receiving country undermines state's capacity to regulate them. It gives rise to economic problem for a state which shows her helplessness to adjust with them. The migrants also do not show absolute loyalty to the government of the receiving country which consequently undermines state's capacity to regulate them. Migrant management is no doubt a greater security challenge for weak and failing states than advanced post-industrial states. Moreover, competition over job, occupation of land coupled with a perceived threat to the local language and culture generates a sense of hostility towards the migrants. Therefore, for a developing state it is not easy to adjust with the migrants as it causes many security challenges. However, the developed states which are capable of formulating and implementing effective migration policies are more secure in the globalised security environment[40].

**Irregular Migration and State Sovereignty:**

Many recent studies have described that irregular migration constitutes a threat to state's sovereignty. This is in the sense that, the states have sovereign right to control their respective borders. And by undermining that control through irregular entry into the destination country, it threatens a state's sovereignty. Koslowski, a security analyst says that irregular migration is "perceived as threat to state's security. Specifically irregular migration and asylum may provide channel for potential terrorists to enter other countries"[41]. It is to be noted that some of the irregular migrants are with criminal intention and not all are criminals and hence are not associated with criminal activities in the receiving countries. Thus care should be taken regarding this point and there should not be generalisation. Misrepresentation of the facts criminalises all migrants crossing the international border.

**Irregular Migration and State's Resources:**

Another security implication of irregular migration is that, it can threaten economic stability by increasing competition among people over employment. These competition, when become severe it enter into political arena and when it becomes politicised lead to group conflict. Many scholars are of the opinion that irregular migration influences the job market of the receiving country. Is has been observed that the skilled migrant workers are ready to work in low prices and also take away job from the hands of the local people. It has also been argued that the migrant threatens the receiving state's social security measures and welfare system. In this context they are viewed as a problem instead of an opportunity. They put pressure on state's welfare system by exploiting them which consequently deteriorate the welfare system of that country. The number of poor migrants is so huge that they create a strong economic threat to the receiving state, which results in shortage in housing and pressurising education capacity. Transportation system, sanitation and communication services are also equally strained. The local communities resent to all these unaccepted development. Both the job sectors, social benefits and welfare services come under serious stress due to such population movement.

**Irregular Migration and Ethnicity, Language and Culture:**

There are numerous examples which expose the link between migration and conflict. For example, few decades' back illegal movement of people from Bangladesh to Northern India has given birth to conflict and confrontation between ethnic groups. Intergroup fighting has also been noticed in Western Europe i.e. between West African immigrants[42]. The Syrian refugee crisis has become an irritating factor which causes anxiety among the member states of the European Union.

Ethnic tension is a potential cause of conflict between migrants and the locals of the destination areas. When the migrants are viewed as 'other' this 'otherness' provoke resentment and ultimately conflict. The competition over job in the receiving places also fuels tension and finally conflict and causes serious law and order problem.

Linguistic and cultural factors are also important factors which results in conflicts in some places. In most of the cases the receiving countries perceive a threat to their distinct culture and language due to the arrival of the migrants in their region. They feel overwhelmed and perceive serious threat to their culture and language. So this uncertainty about the future of their language and culture gives birth to their resentment to the migrants which consequently lead to conflict. The migrants having their distinct cultural identity are seen to be changing the local culture and tradition. And this feeling fuels a sense of hatred towards the migrants.

**Irregular Migration and Demographic Security:**

Demographic security is perceived to be threatened due to illegal migration flow. The original population in the receiving state feels demographically overwhelmed due to heavy migration inflow in their region. They also fear that their population will come to a minimum in comparison to the migrants who in turn will dominate the locals.

**Irregular Migration and Internal Harmony:**

Among the many components of security of a state, the internal harmony and its social stability can be at risk when the flow of migrants takes place. To be clearer, the rise of migrant population who are treated as foreigner in a receiving state consequently hampers the internal harmony, create separate groups and finally racial violence. It is also noticed that the criminal activities among the migrants are severe and higher than the native people.

**Irregular Migration and its Link to Terrorism and Human Rights Violation:**

It is very often accepted that irregular migrants constitutes to be security threat to a Nation's sovereignty. The terrorist network very often recruits from this irregular migrants and expand their network and activities. In the context of India and Bangladesh, this fact has been confirmed by the high officials of Indian Security Forces. Therefore, a host country's counter terrorism policy measures often lead to human rights violation of irregular migrants since all the irregular migrants are not terrorists (Amnesty International, 2008). In fact adequate care should be taken while devising policies by a host nation where migrant influx takes place[43]. In the present world scenario all most all the countries of the world are following strict and restrictive border control policies and are also tightening their visa regulation. Therefore, it is not easy to enter a country with fraudulent documents even for economic needs. It is to be noted that many irregular migration take place for better life and economic employment opportunities in a host country. However, the assumption is that, flawed documentation system may allow the free movement of terrorists and criminals along with economic migrants who enter a state with legal documents. Moreover, tightening of visa regulation may not be helpful for most of the economic migrants to obtain a visa document easily. So the difficulty in getting a proper legal document to enter another country for economic reason forces them to search for illegal route although they do not have any ill intention in a host country. However, strict border control mechanism and checking at the border may subsequently make them vulnerable to human rights violation[44].

## Irregular Migration, Climate Factors and Conflicts:

The Neo Malthusian argues that, climate change in some places will devastate the economies of locals and force many of them to search for new job option. Some of them may seek to migration route in search of job crossing an international border (example the case between India and Bangladesh). In other way the arrival of migrants in a place which is already under climate change related stress will increase tension between locals and the migrants. Population growth results in competition over the resources. And such competition reaches to the point of conflict if the resources are strained under climate change phenomena. In the context of India and Bangladesh, which has a record of apprehension and conflict due to migration, the countries are more susceptible to increase instability. Out of the partition of India in 1947, Pakistan was born and when Pakistan was divided, it gave birth to

Bangladesh in 1971. Migration from Bangladesh has become a factor of tension between India and the former. It has been observed that, an increasing number of environmentally driven migrants are residing in the Indian state over the last decades. Much of this migration took place mainly due to the adverse climate impacts such as flooding in the river and erosion, which caused adverse impacts on agriculture and economies of Bangladesh. As these Bangladeshis see a better economic and better life option in neighbouring country they opt for migrating to India. Thus these regions, where migration influx takes place witness more conflicts and hence are at the peril of future conflict[45].

Many scholars are of the opinion that the socio-economic and political problem or instability in a country forces many of its population to search for a safe haven for them. The Neo-Malthusian are of the opinion that population movement from one place to another crossing the international boundary will be fuelled due to the changing climate condition which is resulting in the devastation of economic condition or livelihood of many people in the affected region. The countries which are located in the climate sensitive regions are prone to greater economic loose. Natural calamities like floods, droughts, cyclones, heat or cold waves etc are going to intensify due to changing climate condition and this generally results in devastation of livelihood of most of the population, who are dependent on agriculture and related sectors. As a response to all these changes in the economy and livelihood, people are forced to migrate especially to those regions where there is better economic option and safe life. However, the irregular crossing of the boundary of a state does not necessarily guarantee them of a safe and secure life. In India a 'Group of Minister Report on Reforming the National Security System' held the view that Bangladeshi migrants illegally residing in India has serious destabilising impacts on the security domain of the country. In the receiving areas the migrants generates social, economic, political, ethnic or communal tensions. They are also in a position to influence the local economies through competition over job, occupation of government's land which generates group conflicts between the locals and the migrants[46].

The illegal settlement of migrants in some areas is also seen as demographic invasion to the destination country. And this fact is noticed in the Indian state of Assam. There started an apprehension among the local people that they will lose their identity due to heavy population increase among the migrants. And consequently they started resenting them which took the form of a violent conflict.

It has also been observed that the migrants themselves form groups to face any attack to them. They start organising into group so as to avert any threat to their existence. Moreover, the enemy neighbouring countries also take benefit from all this phenomena. They try to recruit from the migrants, many anti-nationals and use them against the receiving country.

Resentment to the migrants takes place due to severe competition over resources between the migrants and the locals; when such competition is politicised, it results in the demands for protection of local identity and power, which in turn gives rise to violence and political disturbance and finally threatens the internal peace and security within a country. Moreover, the issue of migration is "regarded by the elites of the receiving country as a danger to the greater political and societal integration, and therefore a security risk. As countries try to restrict the influx of people into their territory, migration gets closely linked with border control, terrorism and criminality, resulting in its securitisation".

"Extreme politicisation of the issue resulted in its securitisation when Bangladeshi illegal migrants were presented as an existential threat to the society, culture, economy and polity of the country" (India).

In short, this theory is:

Migration> competition over resources> local resentment >politicised and takes the form of demand for preservation of local identity>fuelled violence and becomes an internal security issue.

Anna Kicinger, a well known scholar on international security has nicely summarised, in a paper, the migration and security link in the following manner:

"Other dimensions of the migration-security nexus may also be highlighted through specifying the component of security that may be put in danger as a result of migratory movements. In other words, we can try to distinguish which values, protected as components of security, might be threatened by international migration and its consequences. Social stability may be at risk when the inflow of immigrants is combined with the rise of xenophobia, lack of integration; international migration can influence the demographic security (high rates of emigration might deepen the process of declining and aging of population, especially in Central and Eastern European countries); International migration can pose a risk to cultural identity which might be illustrated by the so-called headscarves affair in France as an example or by the rising popularity of extremist right-wing parties in response to high immigration levels; international migration can pose a threat to social security system and welfare state philosophy- people might not be willing to pay high taxes if they do not feel that the other do the same and share the same values which is true in case of economically inactive immigrants and asylum seekers living on social benefits; International migration might be a risk to internal security which is illustrated e.g. by the crime levels among the immigrants that are higher than among the native population; international crime networks dealing in drugs and arms; trafficking in human beings or, last but not least, terrorists using both legal and illegal migration channels to penetrate the country"[47].

## Irregular Migrants and Their Human Rights

After analysing the security implications irregular migrants on the place of destination it is desirable to have a look on the security of those people who crosses an international border even at the risk of their life. In many quarters there has been serious concern regarding the human rights violation of the migrants who crosses an international border without any valid documents or fulfilling the regulatory norms of the sending and the receiving country. Although this research work is primarily concentrated on the study of the security implications of the irregular migrants on the destination country at the same time it is also pertinent to analyse the challenges faced by the migrants in the course of their transit to the destination country. It is relevant, because it involves the issue of human rights of the migrant people and every democratic country of the world is committed to look into the human rights of even foreign nationals. It is true that all the migrants who come to a destination country are not criminals or want to be involved in criminal activities, although some of them can be exploited to be involved in such illegal activities. In spite of all these facts, the migrants have their human rights and dignity. They come to a foreign country with the hope of survival. However, it has been observed in many times that in the course of their transit the migrants face unbearable problems which necessitate the task of having a serious discussion on the human rights and the security of the undocumented migrants.

Various studies on irregular migration pointed out that the irregular migrants very often face harassment, exploitation, sexual abuse and also ill treatment. There has been report of ill treatment by the border guarding forces and especially the women migrants caught at the international border are mostly exploited physically, sexually and economically. Moreover, after their arrival in the foreign country their survival becomes very pathetic as their illegal status makes it very difficult for them to survive.

The following points describe the issues of human rights of the migrants who come to a foreign country through illegal routes.

**Exploitation while Crossing the Border:**

Crossing an international border by illegal means is, no doubt, a painful experience. It has been noticed that for crossing the border the migrants pay to the brokers and also the border police. Women migrants are very often sexually abused which they cannot even resist. Sometimes the brokers and other anti-social elements snatch money from the migrants. Some of these ill-fated people also face violence and death which never come to the limelight. Many human rights organisations have highlighted about this fact. However, little attention has been given to their plights as these migrants are considered irregular who crosses an international border illegally.

**Problem in the Destination Country:**

Many migrant people are successful in crossing an international border despite serious exploitation at the border. In the country of destination, in case they come to the apprehension of being a migrant, they are left in a position of no one's citizen. They cannot stay or even get back as the origin country shows reluctance to accept them as their citizens. Lack of evidence to prove their identity alienate them from the mainstream of society and also deprive them of having an access to the basic welfare services for their survival.

**Exploitation and Exclusion in the Destination Country:**

Most of the migrants are forced to work in informal sectors even at a low wage. As they have no other option of survival in a foreign country they are forced to work in all those sectors where the local workers may refuse to be engaged. They are paid with low salary in return of hard work which causes their economic exploitation. They are even employed in very hazardous sectors without any security of their life. As they are unable to open a bank account to save their earning, very often their money is snatched by local thieves.

**Violation of Human Rights:**

As these migrants enter into a foreign country without any valid documents, they are always ill treated. It has been observed that the women migrants employed as domestic help are not allowed to take leave from their jobs even if they fall ill or want to visit their home. They are even charged heavy rent for their house, so they opt for encroaching government land. The migrants, in the case of their abuse, ill treatment and even violence, do not complain to the police in the fear of being identified and deported. Thus they are forced to lead the life of a life-less object in a foreign country.

After an analysis of all the facts as mentioned above it is clear that, although the migrants cross an international border illegally, but all of them are not criminals or want to be involved in criminal activities in the place of destination. However, their subsequent settlement in the receiving places causes serious problem and they are very often resented by the locals. Increase in migration population gives rise to a community which, in turn, try to perpetuate their position in a foreign country. Even they form groups to resist any perceived threat and hence consequently they get involved in violent acts in a foreign country which is never tolerated and there emerges the demand for their deportation making the situation to become more complicate.

## References

1. United Nations Department of Economic and Social Affairs, Population Division, 2013.
2. Maharana, Ashok Kumar. (2018), "Reshaping India's national security in the face of irregular Bangladeshi migration to India: search for possible solutions" *International Journal of Multidisciplinary Educational Research*, 7: 63-64.

3. Newcombe, E. (2005). Irregular migration: Research, policy and practice, COMPAS, Annual International Conference, July 7-8, 2005. *The International Migration Review,* 39(4), 962-964.

4. Global Commission on International Migration (2005), *Irregular Migration, State Security and Human Security,* University College London.

5. Buzan, B. (2007), *People, states & fear: an agenda for international security studies in the post-cold war era,* Colchester, UK : ECPR Press

6. Wennerhed, Felicia Matz. , "The Securitization of Migrants: A critical discourse analysis of migration in EU policy", [Online: web] Accessed 19 July. 2019 URL: http://lup.lub.lu.se/luur/download?func=downloadFile & recordOId=8873376 & fileOId=8873380.

7. *ibid.*, p. 15.

8. Farny, Elisabeth. (2016), "Implications of the Securitisation of Migration", [Online: web] Accessed 18 July. 2019 URL: https://www.e-ir.info/2016/01/29/implications-of-the-securitisation-of-migration/.

9. Ibrahim, M. (2005), "The Securitization of Migration: A Racial Discourse", *International Migration,* 43(5), 163-187.

10 Wennerhed, Felicia Matz. , "The Securitization of Migrants: A critical discourse analysis of migration in EU policy", [Online: web] Accessed 19 July. 2019 URL: http://lup.lub.lu.se/luur/download?func=downloadFile & recordOId=8873376 & fileOId=8873380.

11. ibid., pp. 21-22.

12. Farny, Elisabeth. (2016), "Implications of the Securitisation of Migration", [Online: web] Accessed 18 July. 2019 URL: https://www.e-ir.info/2016/01/29/implications-of-the-securitisation-of-migration/.

13. ibid., *p. 02.*

14. Das, Pushpita. (2016), *Illegal Migration from Bangladesh: Deportation, Border Fences and Work Permits,* New Delhi: Institute for Defence Studies and Analyses.

15. ibid., p.34.
16. ibid., p. 34.
17. Burrows, Kate and Kinney, Patrick L. (2016), "Exploring the Climate Change, Migration and Conflict Nexus" *International Journal of Environmental Research and Public Health,* 13 (443): 07.
18. *ibid.*, p.07.
19. Atif, Laiq Ahmed. (2013), "Cause of irregular migration" [Online: web] Accessed 6 June. 2019 URL: https://timesofmalta.com/articles/view/Cause-of-irregular-migration.480336.
20. Das, Pushpita. (2016), *Illegal Migration from Bangladesh: Deportation, Border Fences and Work Permits*, New Delhi: Institute for Defence Studies and Analyses.
21. Globalization 101, Pull Factors [Online Web] Accessed 08 July 2019 URL: www.globalization101.org/pull-factors/
22. ibid., *p. 02.*
23. European Asylum Support Office (2016), Significant Pull/Push Factors for Determining of Asylum-Related Migration, Maastricht University and the Global Migration Data Analysis Centre (GMDAC) of the International Organization for Migration, Luxembourg.
24. Czaika, M., & de Haas, H. (2012), "The role of internal and international relative deprivation in global migration", Oxford Development Studies, 40(4), 423-442.
25. Cummings, C., Pacitto, J., Lauro, D., & Foresti, M. (2015), "Why people move: Understanding the drivers and trends of migration to Europe", [Online: web] Accessed 5 July. 2019 URL: http://www.odi.org/sites/odi.org.uk/files/odi-assets/publicationsopinion- files/10208.pdf.
26. European Asylum Support Office (2016), Significant Pull/Push Factors for Determining of Asylum-Related Migration, Maastricht University and the Global Migration Data Analysis Centre (GMDAC) of the International Organization for Migration, Luxembourg.

27. De Haas, H. (2011), "Mediterranean migration futures: Patterns, drivers and scenarios", *Global Environmental Change,* 21(1), S59–S69.

28. Kari, Umar, Malasowe, Godwin, Collins, Ogbu (2018), "A Study of Illegal Migration Trends and the Pull and Push Factors in Nigeria, 2011-2017" *World Journal of Innovative Research* (WJIR), Volume-5, Issue-6, December 2018 Pages 53-60.

29. httpwww.phschool.comatschoolap_miscrubenstein_cultland pdfsCh3_ Issue1.pdf

30. European Asylum Support Office (2016), Significant Pull/Push Factors for Determining of Asylum-Related Migration, Maastricht University and the Global Migration Data Analysis Centre (GMDAC) of the International Organization for Migration, Luxembourg.

31. ibid., p. 28.

32. Das, J., Talukdar, D. (2016), "Socio-Economic and Political Consequence of Illegal Migration into Assam from Bangladesh", *Journal of Tourism & Hospitality, Volume* 5: 04.

33. ibid., p. 04.

34. ibid., p. 04.

35. ibid., p. 04.

36. Hurlock, Karly, (2019), "Political and Economic Impacts of Irregular Migration Across the Indo-Bangla Border", [Online: web] Accessed 11 July 2019. URL: iaffairscanada.com/2019/ political-and-economic-impacts-of-irregular-migration-across-the-indo-bangla-border/

37. Das, J., Talukdar, D. (2016), "Socio-Economic and Political Consequence of Illegal Migration into Assam from Bangladesh", *Journal of Tourism & Hospitality,* Volume 5: 05.

38. Devi, Trishnashree (2018), "Political Impact of Migration in Assam Politics" *The Research Journal of Social Sciences,* volume 9 number 12: 56.

39. ibid., p. 56.

40. Adamson, Fiona B. (2006), Crossing Borders: International

Migration and National Security [Online: web] Accessed 29 March 2019 URL: https://www.mitpressjournals.org/doi/abs/10.1162/isec.2006.31.1.165

41. Global Commission on International Migration (2005), Irregular Migration, State Security and Human Security, University College London.

42. Burrows, Kate and Kinney Patrick L. (2016), "Exploring the Climate Change, Migration & Conflict Nexus" *International Journal of Environmental Research & Public Health*, 13(443): 8

43. Ullah, A K M Ahsan. (2013), Irregular Migrants, Human Rights and Securitization in Malaysia: An Analysis from a Policy Perspective [Online: web] Accessed 29 March 2019 URL: https://link.springer.com/chapter/10.1057/9781137298386_12

44. ibid., p. 179.

45. Burrows, Kate and Kinney, Patrick L. (2016), "Exploring the Climate Change, Migration and Conflict Nexus" *International Journal of Environmental Research & Public Health*, 13(443): 12.

46. Manoharan, N. (2014) "Illegal Migration from Bangladesh: Threat to India's Internal Security" [Online Web] Accessed 10 December 2017 URL: http://bharatkalyan97.blogspot.in/2014/05/illegal-immigrantsfrom-bangladesh.html.

47. Central European Forum for Migration Research (2004), International Migration as a Non-Traditional Security Threat and the EU Responses to This Phenomenon, Warsaw.

# 3

## Irregular Bangladeshis' Migration to India: Factors Responsible

The origin of the migration of the people from one region to another can be traced back to the beginning of the human civilisation. Since the time immemorial human beings have been in search of new places, new region and new environment which can guarantee them a safe and better condition of life. Migration is a phenomenon not only limited to the human being, but birds, animals and other living species have also records of migration in search of new and safe places. Thus the world history is not only characterised by the migration of human being- internally or externally, but also characterised by the movement of all kind of species and such migration may be short term or permanent. Human migrations have always been influenced by several factors which may be noticed either in the place of origin or in the place of destination. Such migration have been taken place in search of a better living condition, availability of adequate food materials or the opportunities to produce them, adequate employment opportunities, better health care system and many others. In the ancient time people were being migrated from one location to another in search of food and shelter, and for safety and security of their life. However, in the beginning of the modern civilisation, migration is influenced by several new factors such as better economic opportunities, educational facilities, better health care system, and most importantly the value of liberal democracy which guarantees them safety and security of life.

In South Asia, India has been the central focus of people of many countries. It also receives the attention of countries all over the world due to its past historical heritage, geographical location, abundance of natural resources and beauty, and more importantly its successful adherence to the ideology of liberal democracy. The French, Dutch, Afghan and British, all came to India in several phases of history. Those movements of outsiders to India had been taken place mainly due to the abundance of resources found to be available in the country. In the last two centuries back India has been a place of destination for many people of its neighbouring countries. There are records of migration of people from Nepal, Myanmar, Pakistan and Bangladesh to India. Thus, in this chapter specific attention have been given to study and analyse the historical background of mass migration from former East Bengal and subsequent Bangladesh to Indian states coupled with its present trend. Moreover attempts have been made to analyse several factors behind Bangladeshis' migration to Indian States.

Irregular entry to the Indian States form countries like Afghanistan, Pakistan, Myanmar, Nepal, Tibet, Sri Lanka, Somalia etc., has been going on since the time immemorial. But what is of serious concern in this connection is the irregular migration of people from Bangladesh to India, because the nature and extent of such migration is much higher in comparison to other States. Besides this, the security ramification of the irregular migration cannot be ignored in the context of India. Millions of migrants from Bangladesh have already entered to India in general and its northeast states in particular. Every day there is taking place cross-border infiltration in the India-Bangladesh border. The long and porous border has made it difficult to arrest the problem. It is also a fact that the geographical location of Bangladesh has devastated the source of livelihood of thousand of Bangladeshis who are, forced to enter into India where they see a ray of hope for their survival. However, linkage of some irregular migrants with Islamic fundamentalist group and terrorist network is dangerous for India. Moreover, population influx into Indian North East particularly Assam has changed its socio-economic and political structure negatively.

Migration of people from East Bengal or East Pakistan which became Bangladesh is not a new phenomenon. Since centuries back it has been going on and has become a perennial problem. People from East Bengal have a record of migration to the North-East part of India since the time of the British rule. Since the beginning of the 19$^{th}$ century A.D., more specifically during the year 1826-27, out migration from Bengal started to the North Eastern part of India like Assam, Tripura, and also to West Bengal. Such migration has been influenced by the factors like better condition of life, employment opportunities, surplus land for agriculture and residence. In the year 1905, Bengal was partitioned into East and West Bengal by the British and in 1912 Assam was carved out as a separate state from East Bengal. In East Bengal the atrocities inflicted by the land lords reduced the poor peasants to the condition of abject poverty and their economic condition was fully broken down. At the same time better economic condition, adequate land, prospects in tea garden attracted many peasants from East Bengal to Assam and West Bengal. Thus in earlier period, migration from East Bengal was in the form of peasant migration. The tea industry developed by the British in India provided the people ample opportunities and consequently attracting many migrants from East Bengal who could work as labourer in the tea garden. Also the partition of India in 1947 gave birth to Pakistan which consisted of East Pakistan and West Pakistan. Such incident, however, produced disastrous consequences in the form of heavy population out flow from East Pakistan to India. Mainly, the religious intolerance and persecution in Pakistan forced huge number of Hindus to migrate to India.

With this, migration from East Pakistan did not stop. Now it is from Bangladesh which came into existence as a separate state in 1971 when Pakistan lost sovereign control over it. The year 1971 and just before it, witnessed a massive population inflow to the Indian states. Suffocated with the religious persecution and atrocities and the indifferent attitude of the government of East Pakistan, millions of Hindu population started pouring in into West Bengal, Assam, Tripura, and other Indian states. After the creation of Bangladesh, migration into India did not stop, rather it acquired a new dimension and it is still going on in various forms. People in earlier times came to Indian States for economic reasons, however in the middle of the 20$^{th}$ century migration from East Bengal is due to a combination of economic, political, religious and other factors. Therefore, in this section of the research attempts have been made to highlight the pattern of migration (mostly irregular) from Bangladesh to India in different phases of history.

## Trends of Irregular Migration from Bangladesh to India

### Colonial Period Migration:

The trend of migration from East Bengal or present Bangladesh started during the colonial rule. Assam came under the British rule in 1826 and then the British established their complete control over it. At that time the British administration required large number of officials to run their administration and hence they started recruiting educated Bengalis as clerks in the bureaucracy[1]. Bangladesh is an agricultural country where one can find millions of landless peasants who had been, through the ages, working in the land of zamindars or land lords. The institution of zamindar was created under 'permanent settlement' system when Lord Cornwallis was the British Governor General in the 18$^{th}$ century. However, the land lords were very oppressive and their exploitation pushed millions of peasants into abject poverty, making it impossible for their survival. Thus they were in search of better condition of life where they can be assured of the minimum needs of food and shelter as it was not possible in their land of birth. Due to such precarious condition there took place migration of large number of landless peasants to Assam as early as in the 19$^{th}$ century itself[2]. Again, the discovery of tea industry in Assam subsequently paved the way for the large scale migration of Bengali Muslims from East Bengal to settle in the river banks all along Brahmaputra valley. An Assamese aristocrat known as Maniram Dutta Barua, who first started the tea plantation influenced the British subsequently. So it was from 1826 to 1840 the tea plantation was started by the British in Assam. As the trade started expanding, they required labourer for working in tea gardens. In such a situation the landless peasants who were in search of better job and good condition of life, started pouring in into Assam region who could be employed as workers in the tea garden. Thereafter, for a century, there took place unabated penetration of Bengali Muslims to Assam region[3].

### *Migration during the Year 1921:*

In the year 1921 the Bengali Muslim migrants completely settled in the Char Island of undivided Golpara district. After their arrival they first occupied the empty islands and then a huge number of new migrants moved to that place. Wherever they found waste land in the district of Goalpara they occupied them and settled there without any trouble. Even the then district revenue staff helped in settling five lakhs of East Bengal Muslims in Assam valley about 25 years[4].

### *Invasion of North East from 1940:*

The real migration or it can be said as the invasion of North East by East Bengal Muslims had commenced from 1940s. It was during that period Assam was being run by a Muslim League ministry under the leadership of Sir Syed Sadaullah. The pro-Muslim attitude of Sadaullah who had an intention to convert Assam into a Muslim majority region helped many Muslim migrants to move towards Assam. The Sadaullah ministry took full advantage of the current situation in East Bengal and Assam and in the name of promoting "Grow more food" scheme thousands of landless Muslim peasants were imported from East Bengal. As a result the Muslim migrants had occupied 1,50,800 acres of land in Assam. Since the intention of Sadaullah was to turn Assam into a Muslim majority region and he was pretending in the name of grow more food scheme, the then Viceroy of India Lord Wavell ridiculed Sadaullah's scheme as "Grow more Muslims" scheme[5].

The number of population influx from East Bengal to the Indian states assumed an outburst as the government and the early incomer clearly encouraged and welcomed fresh migrants. There took place significant increase in population of those areas in Assam where the migrants settled themselves. The census report strictly confirms the fact of increase in population. "The 1911 census report recorded 51,000 persons (mainly Muslims) as born in East Bengal settled in Golpara as against 3,000 persons in the rest of Assam. By 1921, there number increased to 1,41,000 in Golpara and 1,17,000 in the rest of Assam"[6]. This clearly states that the proportion of Muslim community had been steadily increasing to the rest of population since 1881. Moreover, the Muslim population increased to 19 percent in 1931 from the earlier 9 percent in 1921. In 1941 it went to 23 percent[7]. On the whole, by 1941, the Muslim populace outnumbered the Hindu inhabitants by "1,62,000 in the Golpara" district. At the same time the Muslim population in the Barpeta subdivision increased from mere 0.1 percent in 1911 to 49 percent in 1949[8].

## Migration during the Partition of India in 1947

Another wave of large scale migration from the state of East Bengal surfaced with the partition of India in 1947. The year after 15$^{th}$ of August 1947 witnessed communal riots and atrocities against the Hindus and Sikhs in West Pakistan. In other words, the government and the Pakistan army made the life of the Hindus miserable and insecure. The same thing exactly happened in the East Pakistan and consequently millions of Hindu refugees came to Assam and West Bengal. It is to be noted that besides this religious atrocities, cross border movement of people of East Bengal to India searching for an economic opportunities still continued[9].

Post-independent India saw a massive flow of people from East Bengal or East Pakistan to West Bengal, Assam, and other North East states. The census data regarding the growth of population on all those Border States confirms about the fact of heavy population influx. "In the first three decades after independence, Assam shows an overall population growth of around 35-36 percent, way ahead of the national average of around 21-25 percent, indicating a rise of population through migration"[10]. The Registrar General of Census in his report of 1963 accounted the number of such Bangladeshi infiltrators in Assam at around 2,20,691. The genocide in East Pakistan carried out by the military Junta and the Liberation War of 1971 caused a massive flow of refugees whose number could be around 10 million, who entered to India form East Pakistan[11].

Not only Assam but also Tripura and West Bengal saw massive population influx from East Pakistan in the post-independence era. The population in Tripura significantly "increased from 6.39 lakhs to 11.42 lakhs, increasing a growth rate of 78.71 percent which is highest in the country"[12]. In comparison to the migrants' population percentage, the share of tribal population decreased from 53.61 percent in 1941 to 31.50 percent in 1961, which further decreased to 28 percent in 1981[13]. Similar is the case of "West Bengal, the census estimated that between 1951 and 1961, approximately 4.5 lakh migrants from East Pakistan, mostly Hindus entered the State"[14]. "As a result the population of the Hindus in the state registered a marginal increase from 78.45 percent in 1951 to 78.80 percent in 1961. Since the 1960s the population of the Hindus in the State has been steadily declining. The proportion of the Muslims, on the other hand, registered an increase of 0.46 percent in 2001. Between 1991 and 2001, North 24 Praganas,

Murshidabad and Malda, bordering Bangladesh registered a population rise of 22.64 percent, 23.70 percent and 24.77 percent respectively– a growth rate which was higher than the State's average of 17.84 percent. On the whole between 1951 and 2001, while the growth rate of the Hindus was 198.54 percent, the Muslims recorded a growth rate of 310.93 percent. This significant up showing in population growth of the Muslims in the State is attributed to illegal migration from Bangladesh"[15].

Towards the end of 1940s and early 1950s there took place massive influx of people from East Pakistan to India due to the division of India into two independent states– India and Pakistan on the basis of religion. Partition not only divided India into two nations, but its consequence was the emergence of two rival religious groups. It followed riots in both India and Pakistan, mainly between the Hindus and the Muslims which left thousands of people in insecure position. As a result of riots there was huge scale migration from both sides– many Hindus came from Pakistan where as many Muslims left India to enter to Pakistan. In Assam the then Census Superintendent in 1951 stated that the migration of the Hindu refugees from Pakistan during the 1940s is the biggest migration to Assam, India.

To control migration flow from both the sides of India and Pakistan, a pact was signed between the first Prime Minister of Independent India Pt. Jawaharlal Nehru, and the first Prime Minister of Pakistan Liaquat Ali Khan. The pact was known as "Nehru-Liaquat Pact" signed on 8$^{th}$ April 1950. This pact re-established some coolness among the minority communities in both parts of the countries as a result of which population influx in both the countries reduced to some extent. The basic objective of the pact was to lessen the fear among the religious minorities of both the sides, to maintain mutual peace and to create an amicable atmosphere where both the countries could discuss their mutual differences to reach to a peaceful solution. According to this agreement the governments of both the countries decided to grant their religious minorities' full equality of citizenship, right of full security, right to protect and maintain their culture, property and personal honour. In a nutshell, the agreement granted fundamental human rights to the religious minority groups residing in India and Pakistan. As a result of this pact, there took place normalcy in India and Pakistan and it significantly ceased migrant influx. Around six lakhs "migrant people were sent back to East Pakistan, largely from Assam" [16]and this was no doubt a positive impact of the pact.

## Migration During 1965, India-Pakistan War

The India-Pakistan War of 1965 which revolved round on the Kashmir issue resulted in large number of people fleeing to India mostly from East-Pakistan. As Assam and West Bengal shares border with Bangladesh, these two Indian states became the major destination for the refugees. According to S. Hazarika, in 1960s around one million people entered India illegally, out of which 9,20,000 were Hindus[17].

## Migration in 1971

The next big influx of people of Bangladesh took place during the 'Liberation War of Bangladesh'. According to various estimates at both official and non official level, about ten million people crossed over to Assam during the war and most of them did not go back after the war ended[18]. Thousands of migrants during this period came via Dhubri got down virtually at every railway station, including the Udalaguri and Darrang district of the state.

### Migration After 1971 War:

After the formation of Pakistan in 1947, the central leadership in the West Pakistan made East Pakistan a subservient region of the former. The newly formed country was also unable to develop its infrastructure to fulfil the needs of its growing population. There took place extensive economic as well as political biases and discrimination and the suppression of the Bengali culture and the linguistic heritage in the East Pakistan. This gave rise to dissatisfaction among the people of East Pakistan with the central government as they felt neglected and discriminated. As a result of such frustration these people joined forces with Sheikh Mujibur Rahman and his Awami League Party which won a landslide victory during the election of 1970. However, the then political leadership was reluctant to accept a Prime Minister from East Pakistan. This consequently gave birth to a civil war or grave internal disturbances in Pakistan in 1970, where the East Pakistan wing demanded a greater autonomy. The civil war "resulted in genocide, and about one to two million people in Bangladesh at that time were killed and 200,000 girls and women were ill treated and about 10 million people crossed the border and took refuge in India"[19].

The genocide perpetrated by the Pakistan army forced millions of people to migrate especially to India. The government of India was faced with the crisis of refugee inflow from East Pakistan side– the largest refugee flow in that time in the world. Refugee camps were set up at the bordering states like West Bengal, Assam, Meghalaya and Tripura. Around 300 refugee camps were established in those bordering states[20].

Due to such refugee flow into India, the central leadership of the country decided to send army to fight "along with the allied force of Mukti Bahini (Freedom Fighter) who defeated the army of Pakistan in a two weak war and Bangladesh, a new country was born out of Pakistan"[21]. Even after the creation of a separate state of Bangladesh, migration from the country to Indian States continued unabated and is still going on. The central government and the state government of Assam and West Bengal seemed to be passive to recognise the problem. Even in many cases some State leadership openly declared that there are no migrants present in their respective States and hence there is no need of identification and deportation of any individual. However, the National Democratic Alliance (NDA) under the Bharatiya Janta Party (BJP), after coming into power at the Centre wining the 2014 general election, has taken several steps to identify the irregular migrants in the Indian States especially in Assam. The implementation of the National Register of Citizens (NRC) in Assam is the case in point.

Just before 1971 in East Pakistan the government kept lakhs of Bihari Muslims who could help the government in controlling the Bangladeshis. After the end of the war around six lakhs of them left Bangladesh. These Bihari Muslims had desired to go back to Pakistan but the Pakistan government did not allow them to enter. At the same time new Bangladesh government and Bengali speaking Bangladeshis did not like them to continue to remain in Bangladesh. As a result these Bihari Muslims along with their families entered India in Maldah, West Dinajpur, Silliguri border crossing Mahananda River and land border, day and night from 1972 to 1975.

**Hindu Migrants After 1971 War:**

Illegal entry of Bangladeshis did not stop even after 1971. There took place migration of Hindu population in several phases to India. These migrants left their landed properties and all materials in Bangladesh and came to settle permanently in India. Their main destination was West Bengal because of the religious and linguistic similarities. Absence of any strict protection system at the international border coupled with homogeneous culture, ethnicity, and social bond helped these Hindu migrants to enter and settle in West Bengal. By 1975 these Hindu migrants were settled in West Bengal[22].

**Muslim Migrants After 1971:**

After Bangladesh was formed in 1971, migration of Muslim population to Indian states continued. The influx of Muslim migrants was, thus, reported more so after 1971 and again in 1975, after the assassination of Sheikh Mujibur Rehman. One cannot compare the Muslim migrants with the Hindu migrants as their intention differs significantly. The Muslim migrants came with an ulterior motive and penetrated through border of Assam, Meghalaya and Tripura with Bangladesh[23].

Bertil Linter refers to another wave of migration in his work 'Great Game East' in the following words: 'A third campaign against Hindu minority began in 2001, as Islamic fundamentalists went on rampage through non-Muslim communities. Thousands of people fled to India'[24]. Bangladesh has now converted itself into Islamic state after bringing necessary changes in its structure. It has always shown indifferent attitudes towards the religious minorities mainly to the Hindus. Thus the Hindus are not in a safe position and apprehend several dangers not only from the Muslim fundamentalist but also from the government. Thus they are forced to migrate into India for security reason. And as such the percentage of the Hindu population has been decreasing day-by-day there. The Hindu population in East Pakistan which was 27 percent in 1947 was reduced to 14 percent in 1971, to 10 percent in 1991, and perhaps by now there would be hardly 5 percent of Hindus in Bangladesh[25].

Ramachandra Guha in his book '*India after Gandhi*' mentions that the number of voters in the electoral rolls of Assam jumped from 6.6 million to 9 million in the decade of 1970s which is due to the migration from Bangladesh. Thus the increase of population in the electoral roll of Assam is the clear indicator of the fact that illegal migration to the state of Assam is still going on in rapid pace. Not only Assam but also Tripura, West Bengal, Manipur and other North East states face the same situation. In a nutshell it can be said that, irregular migration continues unabated which has its origin in the British rule in India.

## Migration to Other Indian Cities

The first choice of the Bangladeshi migrants in India is no doubt the North East states and West Bengal. However they also shift their attention to other Indian states and decide to migrate to all those states when they are met with resistance along with insufficient resources in the state of their first choice. In other words, irregular population influx into the state of West Bengal, Assam, and other North East states caused scarcity of land for agriculture. It also increased competition in low skilled and unskilled job sectors in these states. As a result the new migrants are pushed to other city centres of India like Delhi, Mumbai, Benguluru, Ahmadabad, Chennai, Odisha and many other regions. All these cities have witnessed the presence of undocumented Bangladeshis who are found to be present in unskilled labour markets and also provides other cheap source of labour and works as house maid, shop keeper etc. In many cases their presences have been noticed and many of them have been arrested by the local police or the law enforcing agencies. The "Gujarat police identified and deported 440 Bangladeshis who were illegally staying in Ahmadabad since 2009"[26]. Similarly "the Delhi Police claimed to have deported more than 45,000 Bangladeshis who were illegally staying in the national capital since 1991"[27]. In 1998 the police agency of Mumbai met resistance in Kolkata when it tried to deport illegal Bangladeshi migrants[28].

Earlier the trend of Bangladeshi migration to other states of India (besides North East and West Bengal) was not so given due attention. However, since the late 1980s such migration trend has been increasingly noticed. Uttar Pradesh, Bihar, Odisha, Gujarat, Karnataka, Tamil Nadu and Kerala, all these states have become now a place of destination of the migrants who illegally cross India-Bangladesh border to enter India. It has been reported that "in 2010, around 8,500 Bangladeshis were illegally staying in Uttar Pradesh out of these 8,500 migrants, 6000 were living in Meerut, 1,800 in Lucknow and

350 in Noida"[29]. Illegal presence of Bangladeshi migrants has also been noticed in many districts of Bihar. In 2013 "around 6,000 persons were accused of being Bangladeshis in Bihar and were handed over notices to prove their Indian citizenship or leave India"[30]. The affected districts in Bihar are Katihar, Kishanganj and Purnea. The state of Odisha is also not free from the presence of irregular Bangladeshi migrants whose presence can be noticed in the districts of Kendrapara, Jagatsinghpur, Malkangiri and Bhadrak. In 2013, the "Odisha government identified nearly 4,000 Bangladeshis in the state" [31] who were illegally staying in many districts.

In a nut shell, irregular migrant population have spread to all over India. They are not only limited to the North Eastern part or West Bengal, but they have also spread to all most all states of India. However, their presence in the Indian State is objectionable due to its security implications for India. Moreover, pressure on demography, ecosystem, environment, land and competition over jobs between migrants and the local population has destabilising outcome. Thus irregular migration needs to be securitised and there is need to devote more energy to tackle the problem.

## Tourism Route to Enter India

Since the last few years of this 21st century, many security analysts have found that the number of Bangladeshi who entered India illegally is decreasing. Today there are many instances where the Bangladeshis are entering India through proper legal procedures. To be more specific they have chosen to tourist route to enter India (which is a legal route). But the problem is that, most of them have never returned to their home land. According to existing source of Government of India, the number of Bangladeshi tourists has doubled in the last two years. Even the security agencies in India have expressed concern over the consistent and sudden spike of tourist's arrival in the last few years. The New Indian Express on 20th January,

2018 reports that 9.4 lakh Bangladeshi tourists came to India in 2014 where as in 2015 the number went up to 11.3 lakh, 13.8 lakh in 2016 and 21 lakh in 2017. Thus in 2017 the number went sharply by 50 percent which reminds us the magnitude of migration to India[32].

No doubt, the tourism industry in India gets profit from such movement. However, non-return of the Bangladeshis tourists have given birth to new concerns in India. Although the Bangladeshi migrants are entering into India through legal route (tourists visas), but many of them do not return to their country and generally overstay illegally. A senior Border Security Force (BSF) official said that, "The main concern is that many Bangladeshi nationals who arrive here on tourist visa do not return and generally overstay illegally", adding that this tourists visa is being misused by several Bangladeshi nationals to enter India with no intention to return back[33].

Thus the number of Bangladeshis crossing India-Bangladesh border illegally to enter India has reduced considerably now. Most of them prefer to legal channel to enter India. The number of Bangladeshi caught crossing the border went down from 3,426 in 2015 to 175 in 2017[34].

## Accounts of Irregular Migrants in India

There is lack of reliable official data on the quantity of irregular Bangladeshi infiltrators present in the state of India. This is because the migrants enter into India clandestinely or surreptitiously. Thus it seems to be impossible to obtain a clear statistics on the Bangladeshis who are staying illegally in different parts of India. In spite of these problems the Indian government has regularly provided information on the number of Bangladeshis who are illegally staying in India. In "1992 the Ministry of Home Affairs (MHA) revealed that till 1991, more than 7 lakh Bangladeshis were identified as staying illegally in different border"[35] states of the country. "The break up the data being: West Bengal, 2,40,446; Assam, 1,35,656; Meghalaya,

14,268; Tripura, 29,382; and Mizoram, 3,18,731"[36]. According to a new revelation made in the Parliament by the then Home Minister of India, Mr. Inderjit Gupta, 10 million irregular migrants from Bangladesh found to be living in India. The India Today magazine in its August 10, 1998 issue "gave the details as follows:

| | | |
|---|---|---|
| Assam | : | 4 million; |
| Bihar | : | 0.5 million; |
| Delhi | : | 0.3 million |
| Maharashtra | : | 0.5 million; |
| Rajasthan | : | 0.5 million; |
| Tripura | : | 0.8 million; |
| West Bengal | : | 5.4 million; |
| Total | : | 10.83 million"[37]. |

Coming to the 21st century, many institutions of the Government of India have given statistics on the number of irregular Bangladeshis in India. In 2004, the Task Force on the Border Management, clarified in the Upper House of the Parliament that till December 2001, around 12 millions irregular "Bangladeshi migrants were staying in the country, including 5 million in Assam and 5.7 million in West Bengal"[38].

However, such announcement was subsequently withdrawn. Apart from the above mentioned case it has also been widely observed that a large number of migrants, who came to India with valid documents and through proper government channel, subsequently did not return even after the expiry of their visa terms and hence continues to reside in the Indian states. Thus they have already become irregular migrants in India whose number crosses millions of population. "According to a government data, between 1972 and 1997, a total of 9,91,031 Bangladeshis entered India with valid documents but did not return"[39]. A new report on visa violators confirms that till "December 31, 2012, approximately 16,350

Bangladeshis who came on valid travel documents were overstaying in India"[40].

## Factors Responsible for Bangladeshis' Migration to India

Migration from Bangladesh to India through illegal means has become a serious problem today. In the previous section of this chapter a detailed analysis has been made regarding the trends and pattern of this migration. In this section attempts have been made to find out the key determinants or factors of irregular Bangladeshis' migration to India.

Crossing the international border through illegal means and to enter India from Bangladesh is the outcome of multiple factors. During the British rule in India, the migration from East Bengal was only for economic reason. In other words there took place migration of thousands of peasants who were to work in the tea industries promoted by the British in the state of Assam. Subsequently, after the creation of separate state of Pakistan the migration was mainly due to religious persecution. Even after the formation of the independent state of Bangladesh religious atrocities against the minority communities continued which forced the minority group to leave the country and to move towards India.

Migration from Bangladesh still continue unabated and what is a matter of concern is, the current flow of migrants who illegally crosses as well as settle in many states of India. Thus migration from Bangladesh to Indian states is not only influenced by any single factor or determinant, but a multiple of factors work behind it. These factors can be brought under the pull and push factors of migration. In this context, the push factors are those which forces many Bangladeshis to leave their country where as the pull factors attracts the migrants to the place of destination i.e. India. Better economic conditions, better wages, better living standard, educational opportunities, health facilities, safety and security, and other welfare schemes in the destination country i.e. India have always attracted the Bangladeshis. On the other hand state atrocities against ethnic and religious minorities mainly the Hindus and weak economic condition coupled with the increasing population density have forced many people of Bangladesh to search for a safe heaven and in this connection the neighbouring country India has always been seen as a place which could help them to get rid of their predicaments.

In the present time a major push factors of Bangladeshis' migration to India has been noticed and there has also been demands in many quarters to securitize such factor i. e. Climate Change. Changing climate conditions in Bangladesh has made its people vulnerable to many natural and environmental hazards. Bangladesh is faced with periodic floods, cyclones, as well as severe droughts every year, which devastate agriculture, economy and livelihood of millions of its people who are dependent upon agriculture or climate sensitive ecosystem. This phenomenon has left millions of Bangladeshis in poverty and unemployment. As a consequence these people see a ray of hope in India where they think that they can survive at least. Finally they cross over international border to enter India.

Thus the continuous and unending flow of Bangladeshi migrants to Assam and other states of India may be attributed to several factors in Bangladesh like, weak economic condition, population growth due to polygamous practice and child marriage, presence of fundamentalist elements, religious and ethnic persecution and most importantly environmental factors like global warming and climate change. Also the demand for working labour class in India attracts many unskilled and low skilled labourers from Bangladesh to the country. Moreover, the porous India-Bangladesh border and non-availability of correct Electoral Roll (ER) and the non completion of the National Register of Citizens (NRC) in the past are the additional factors of illegal Bangladeshis' infiltration to India[41].

It is to be noted that migrants from Bangladesh who entered India illegally are categorised as irregular migrant who belonged to both Hindu and Muslim community including others. However, the reasons behind migration of Hindu people from Bangladesh differ from that of migration of Muslim population. In other words, it is mainly due to religious persecution and state apathy many Hindu people migrated to India. Thus their main intention was to protect their life in the face of organised crimes against them. Although some people from Bangladesh from Hindu community crossed over to Indian states due to economic reasons but the basic compelling factor was the religious intolerance and atrocities. And this is clear from the fact that the percentage of Hindu population has been reduced to a minimum in Bangladesh now. On the other hand, it is the deteriorating economic conditions followed by unemployment, loose of job, weak standard of life have forced the people from Muslim community to enter India. Bangladesh has converted itself into a religious based country with Islam as its state's religion and there is no question of religious atrocities against the Muslim community there. Thus religious persecution is not at all a ground behind migration of Muslim people from Bangladesh. In other words, the push factor behind migration of people from Muslim community has been the economic one. They see better employment opportunities, better standard of living, better health and education facilities along with safety, security and peace in India.

The following section proceeds with a discussion on several key determinants or factors responsible for irregular migration to Indian states of Assam, other north eastern states and other states of India. In other words socio-economic, political and environmental forces in their home country or personal desire of an individual influence their decisions to migrate to the neighbouring India. Mainly factors like political instability, atrocities against religious and ethnic minorities, social insecurity, economic stagnation and inadequate employment opportunities, population growth and most important changing climate conditions and its resultant impact upon the life and livelihood of Bangladeshi population have forced them to leave their homes and migrate to India.

**Political Factors: State's Persecution:**

It is well known that East Bengal or East Pakistan which became Bangladesh in 1971, has not been able to treat its religious and ethnic minorities equally and there has been many instances of state's organised atrocities, oppression and injustice done to them, which has forced its minority sections mainly the Hindus to leave the country. The oppression of the Hindu community in the then East Bengal (East Pakistan) can be dated back to 1950s and 1960s. A communal riot took place in the Khulna district of East Pakistan in 1950 against the Hindu minority which can be the worst case of the state's organised persecution against the minority Hindu. The riot took the life of thousands of Hindus as a result of which lakhs of them fled to India to save their life. Around 7.5 lakh Hindu migrants took shelter in West Bengal within just three months beginning from May to July 1950[42].

Thus religious intolerance has forced many Hindus to leave the country and to move to India. East Pakistan has never accepted secularism as the foundation of a peaceful state, rather it has in many times adhered the policy of religious discrimination which has not only affected its unity and integrity but also political stability. Throughout the 1950s the Hindus were forced to leave East Pakistan and it continued due to state's orchestrated persecution against such community. According to a data of the Ministry of Home Affair, between 1946 and March 1958, 41.17 lakhs migrants came to India from which 32.32 lakhs were established in West Bengal[43].

The communal riot in East Pakistan and the India-Pakistan War of 1965 were important push factors forcing a large number of Hindus to migrate to India. The fundamentalist section of

Bangladesh found an opportunity to burst against the minority as the government of the state was not secular. These sections, rather, got helps from the state to conduct such violence against the minority community. Moreover, during the Liberation war of Bangladesh in 1971, another massive out-migration from East-Pakistan took place "when the Pakistani military establishment tried to suppress Bengali nationalism through the brutal military force"[44]. It is estimated that around 10 million persons including 6.7 million Hindus[45] entered India as refugees.

Bangladesh emerged as an independent country in 1971 as a secular country, but it could not help the Hindu minority there. Although the constitution was secular in form, but its political leader were not able to adhere the principle of secularism in true spirit. With the emergence of General Zia-ur-Rahamn who declared himself as the President of Bangladesh on the 28th April 1977, the principle of secularism was given a goodbye. Subsequently, he converted Bangladesh into a religious based state and hence promoted religious intolerance[46]. And this witnessed another period of hostility against the Hindus which consequently forced thousands of Hindus to leave Bangladesh and to move to India.

Thus the year after 1975 saw the Islamisation of the Bangladesh constitution which was given effect during the military regime of General Zia and General Ershad. Such a move by the military not only increased anxieties among the Hindu population but also made it impossible for them to stay there in an atmosphere of imminent danger to their life and liberty. The communal forces and the religious fundamentalists in Bangladesh got support and were strengthened when Islam was formally declared as the state religion in 1988 through 8th amendment of the constitution[47]. It encouraged the communal elements and Islam emerged as an important factor in politics which influenced the state's affair. No doubt the general populace positively responded the concept of "Islamic State" but other minorities mainly the Hindus were seriously ignored and witnessed torture of many kinds. It also gave rise to many religious fundamentalism, communal violence and destruction of temples of Hindu community. The Islamisation of Bangladesh had also its international ramification. During the Ram Janambhoomi-Babri Masjid issue in India, there was destruction of many temples in Bangladesh especially in1989, 1990 and 1992[48]. Even in the beginning of the 21st century and the ushering of democracy in Bangladesh, religious atrocities and riots has not been stopped. The Bangladesh National Party (BNP) and its ally, Jamat-e-Islami continued to torture, harass and ill-treat the Hindus there.

Persecution of Hindu was at its peak at the time of the Liberation War of Bangladesh. According to an estimate, at that time approximately 30,00,000 people from Hindu community were butch in the largest genocides in the country. The 'Time' magazine on 2nd August 1971 reported that the Hindus, who account for three-forth of the refugees, and a majority of dead, have borne the brunt of the Muslim military hatred. According to the BBC, 9th March 2013 "Official estimates say more than three million were killed and tens of thousands of women raped during the Bangladesh's secession". Many leaders from the Hindu community in Bangladesh are of the opinion that attacks against the Hindus in that country are carried out not only by the hardliner Islamists but also supporters of political parties including the Awami League and the Bangladesh Nationalist Party. The main objective of conducting such violence against the Hindu community is to grab their land and other property with the help of several acts. Due to such pre planned atrocities, many Hindus have left Bangladesh and fled to India to escape harassment, intimidation and violence[49].

The statement of the Executive Director, Amity for Peace, Bangladesh, Salam Azad, receives greater attention here, he states that after Bangladesh became a theocratic state, having a great departure from the principle of secularism and democracy, the marginal section particularly the Hindu community were treated as the unwanted low rank citizens in their own nation. The judiciary also hardly helps them in getting justice. Many Non Governmental Organisations (NGOs) in Bangladesh have stepped forward for the protection of the right s of Hindu population there, but all attempts have been fruitless[50].

In the Post-election violence in Bangladesh especially of 1991, 2001 and 2014, the Hindus were the main target. Moreover, emergence of Islamic terrorist faction like the Harkat-ul-Jihad-ul-Islami (HUJI) and others have created a situation of fear and hostility against the religious minorities. There have also been many instances of attack against the secular intellectuals and journalists by these terrorist groups[51]. Thus in contrast to the ideology of Awami-League which supports 'Liberal Secular Values' the BNP and its allies Jamat-e-Islami and Islamic Okiyo Jote always fuels religious intolerance[52].

The socio-political environment in Bangladesh since its creation has not been favourable for the Hindu and other minority communities. It has not only perpetuated religious discrimination and atrocities against such communities but also dispossessed them of their movable and immovable property leaving them in abysmal poverty and backwardness. In the present scenario, the Hindus are also unable to get a suitable job due to stiff competition with the majority community there. Moreover, they are also not getting job as daily wage labourer. The religious divide of the country always take the side of the Muslim community which has pushed many Hindus and even the Buddhist from Bangladesh to other countries[53].

### *Land Alienation: Another Form of State's Persecution*

State repression in East Bengal was not only limited to conduct violent activities against the religious minorities. Discriminatory land laws enacted in East Bengal in "1947 such as East Bengal Requisition of Property Act of 1948, the East Bengal Evacuees (Administration of Immovable Property) Act of 1951 and the East Pakistan Disturbed Persons Rehabilitation

Ordinance of 1964"[54] were some important laws which enabled the state to intervene, manage and transfer the property of people who were displaced by communal violence. These legislations necessarily manifest State's hidden agenda to eliminate the Hindu minority from the state i.e. first to promote communal riot and then capture their property through these laws. The corrupt administrators started manipulating all those laws and dispossessed and alienated the Hindus from their movable and movable assets and property.

In 1972, the newly formed government in Bangladesh brought a promulgation known as the 'Bangladesh Vesting of Property and Assets Order'. The order provided that the assets left by the Pakistani and other displaced individuals shall be treated as one division. The subsequent move of the government to repeal the previous act in 1976 enabled it to administer, manage, dispose and transfer such properties[55]. Those laws dispossessed a person from his property and subsequently forced them to migrate. It has been estimated that "between 1965 and 2006, approximately 1.2 million Hindu households or 6 million Hindus were directly and severely affected by the Enemy/Vested Property Act and lost 2.6 million acres of land"[56]. Another study on the causes and consequences of implementation of the Vested Property Act made it clear that approximately one million Hindus households have been dispossessed of over 1.64 million acres of landed property[57].

### *Violence against Hindu Minority in Recent Year in Bangladesh:*

The minority Hindu in Bangladesh have always faced the ire of several fundamentalists group supported by the government machinery. The election of 2014 witnessed yet another instances of attacks against the Hindus there. "Soon after the voting ended in Bangladesh, the Hindu had to face the ire of the activist of Bangladesh National Party and Jammat-Shibir. Hindu houses have been looted, vandalized and burned in several places like Thakugaon, Dinajpur, Rangpur, Bogra,

Lalmonirhat, Rajshahi, Chittagong and Jessore"[58]. Similarly the miscreants attacked the Hindu localities, temples, business establishments in several parts of Bangladesh where the Hindus were staying after the national election[59]. The main reason behind attack against the Hindus in all those areas at that time was the rejection by Hindu community to boycott the election which was imposed by Jammat-Shibir activists in Bangladesh. Hundred of houses were vandalised and even there were instances of explosion of 250 bombs[60].

Violence against the Hindus did not stop after 2014 general election and there have been many instances of attacks against the Hindus. Many time false rumours have caused serious attacks against this community. On "May 2014, a mob of nearly 3,000 people attacked Hindu households and temples in eastern Bangladesh after two youths from the community allegedly insulted the Prophet Muhammad on Facebook at Homna in Comilla district"[61]. The editor of Hindu Existence said that "Minority Hindus are attacked again and again in Bangladesh on false rumours of defaming Muhammad in face book. In most of the cases, it is established that some Muslim perpetrators like to use the social media like facebook to upload objectionable comments and pictures against Islam and Muhammad in a very motivated way. After spreading rumours of blasphemy or defamation of Muhammad the Islamic goons attack Hindus, Hindu-households, temples and specially the women folk"[62]. Thus, even today the minority community faces continuous discrimination, atrocities and violence perpetuated by many fundamentalist groups and supported by many political parties in Bangladesh. All these persecutions have been forcing the community to leave Bangladesh and to search for a safe place which they see in India.

***Hindus and other Minorities Forced to Leave Bangladesh:***

State's apathy to the problem of Hindus in Bangladesh has encouraged the fundamentalists and anti-Hindu political parties to conduct violence against the minority communities. The main objective of such kind of violent behaviour and assault is to snatch the lands and other properties of Hindu people. Jyotirmoy Barua, a Supreme Court lawyer in the capital Dhaka, once observed "When we say it's just political, it legitimizes the violence. Most of the people's houses they are burning are poor. If you burn their house, they will leave the country, and you get their land"[63]. By the misuse of the Vested Property Act which remained in force until 2001, the government in Bangladesh expropriate "enemy" (in practice the Hindu) lands. Thus millions of acres of land were seized by the government which left almost all Hindus in the country landless. It is to be noted that lack of employment opportunities in other sectors compel the people to be dependent upon agriculture practice for which agricultural land is required. Thus land is the main source of livelihood and for it there takes place many competitions and the successive government also helped in grabbing the land of Hindus to satisfy the majority of people of influential community. Most of the Hindus and other social scientists are of the opinion that land is the major reason for which they have been attacked historically and it is still going on[64].

**Economic Factors:**

Besides religious persecution against the minority community in Bangladesh, several economic factors have pushed and continue to do so millions of Bangladeshis to migrate to the neighbouring India. It is to be noted that weak economic conditions in Bangladesh has forced both the Hindus and Muslims to opt for migration to the Indian States.

Since its emergence as a separate independent State, Bangladesh has not been able to meet the needs and aspirations of its increasing population. During the British rule there was exploitation of the poor agricultural workers in the hands of the zamindars as a result of which there took place migration of East Bengali people to the Assam region. Such trend has assumed a new dimension today with unabated population inflow to the Indian States. The uneven distribution of agricultural land has pushed the labourer into abysmal poverty. Moreover, the weak industrialisation in Bangladesh has not been able to generate adequate jobs for the locals. Adding to this problem, the increasing population has already put pressure on the agricultural sector, which has not been able to meet the production target and to feed its increasing population. Again, the unsustainable agricultural practice has degraded the soil quality. Seasonal floods and droughts are other factors which results in devastation of agriculture. To be more specific, weak economic condition due to poor agricultural practice and slow industrialisation has resulted in large scale unemployment and consequently poverty and backwardness. And as such the affected people in Bangladesh find no other alternatives but to enter into neighbouring India where they see ample job opportunities and a stable economic condition.

Thus a variety of economic factors as mentioned below have acted as major push factors in forcing the Bangladeshi people, form Hindu and Muslim communities, to leave their own country and to illegally enter into India.

***Weak Employment Opportunities:***

The implementation of the Enemy/Vested Property Act dispossessed a large number of Hindus of their ancestral property and land whereas the increased population, climate hazards and disasters are responsible for alienating a large section of people in Bangladesh from their agricultural land. Bangladesh is an agricultural dominated country where 60 percent of its land is under agriculture[65]. The contribution of agriculture to the GDP is 17 percent and it also gives employment to more than 45 percent of the total labour force[66]. Although, agricultural practice in Bangladesh has increased, it is not at par with the increasing population. In 1974 its population was 70.88 million where as it reached to 159.80

million in 2011[67]. Thus the agricultural output is not sufficient to meet the demands of its increasing population. Use of fertilisers, pesticides etc no doubt increases the production but its negative effect cannot be denied. It has deprived the soil from needed organic matter which has led to land degradation and low productivity. Therefore the agricultural workers in the rural areas are forced to migrate as there is no other suitable option to earn their livelihood in their home country.

It is to be noted that Bangladesh is a heavily populated country in the world. Due to increasing population along with reduced land size, the farms lands are becoming fragmented into smaller land holdings. One of the obvious outcome of the small land holding is the small agricultural out-puts, which cannot meet the needs of a family throughout the year. In other words the big size of a family with small agricultural land makes it very difficult to meet the economic needs of the family the year around. Moreover, the vulnerability of the Bangladeshi farmers to seasonal floods and droughts is another reason for migration decision. These environmental disasters results in scarcity and famine which consequently triggers out-migration[68]. The floods of July 1974 in Bangladesh have forced many poor and landless to migrate to adjacent state, West Bengal. Between July 1974 and March 1975 the Border Security Force (BSF) of India intercepted around "39,000 Bangladeshis who were trying to enter India"[69].

***Weak Industrialisation:***

Industrialisation is essential for the economic development of a country as gives rise to employment opportunities and consequently alleviate poverty. It also contributes to the GDP of a country and provides consumer goods and capital goods. Bangladesh, is however, not so strong in the industrialisation index. It has not been able to employ the "higher proportion of working-age population, with labour force increasing at the rate of 3.39 percent per annum"[70]. In other words, industrialisation in Bangladesh has not been able go along with the increasing labour force. Thus the working age group people look outside for employment as there are no adequate opportunities to be employed in their own country. It is a matter of surprise that the Bangladeshi leadership does not seem to be interested in devising new schemes for employment generation in order to employ its unskilled labourers who are finally forced to cross the international boundary to enter India illegally with the hope of a better avenue for job. Thus the unskilled and low skilled labourer moved to India not merely as an answer to the labour demand in India but for their survival. In a nutshell, illegal entry to the Indian States "from Bangladesh is a self rescue migration that is, fleeing from poverty, hunger, political and religious persecution, governmental apathy and dark future in Bangladesh"[71].

Thus, mostly the Bangladeshi people decide to go out due to economic reason. The scarce resources, unemployment and poverty have pushed many of them to India. The basic needs of food, clothing and shelter is not available adequately there and the people also do not get better wages to sustain their family[72]. In contrast, the economic opportunities in India acts as pull factor and continue to attract the Bangladeshis towards the country. At various places in India they could purchase agricultural land for cultivation. They also get appointment as daily labourer, contract labourer with good wages. In other word, the vast economic opportunities in India assure them of livelihood and job security. Ladies are also employed as tailors, shopkeepers apart from working as helps in labour markets and household. They are also employed in cultivation and related sectors. In a nutshell, a good income with minimum risk has attracted and continues attracts millions of people from Bangladesh to enter India clandestinely[73].

In the context of Assam, the region has always been an attracting place for the Bangladeshi people. Due to certain internal factors in Assam, the Bangladeshis have got the opportunities to enter as well as settle in Assam. The job avenues in Assam become very wide as the local Assamese are not interested to be engaged in rural sectors for self-employment. The poor work culture and the easy going habit found among the young generation in Assam have provided ample scope for employment of irregular migrants from Bangladesh. This also creates new job avenues for the new or fresh infiltrators[74]. This trend has, therefore, employed millions of infiltrators in Assam whereas left the locals jobless. In other word the lured for a salaried job is an important factor behind the growth of poor work culture and unemployment among the local Assamese. Many Assamese youth have preferred to go out-side for a paltry salary of rupees of seven thousand or so instead of concentrating on locally available rural economic sectors[75]. The consequence is clear and if one ask that why there are 23 lakhs of unemployed person in Assam, then the answer would be- how it is possible for millions of infiltrators to find job in the state[76]? Notably the Bangladeshi migrants are ready to be occupied in manual work sector in Assam. They are ready to work as rickshaw pullers, house construction workers, house painters, gardeners, field workers, road construction labourer, vegetable vendors etc. and women migrants mostly work as house maid. The most important thing is that these migrants are very hard working and show readiness to work in abnormal hours and in very difficult activities which the locals Assamese worker are not willing to do. Thus the availability of adequate space in work sectors in Assam attracts the poor segments of Bangladeshi society to the state of Assam even at the risk of illegal entry to the state[77].

After entering to India illegally most of the migrants from Bangladesh become successful in obtaining Indian citizenship i.e. they obtain voter identity card or even other supporting documents. By providing all those documents they get employment even in government's programmes launched for poverty eradication through employment. Schemes launched by the Central Government like the National Rural Employment Guarantee Schemes (NREGS) and the National Rural Health Mission (NRHM) immensely benefits all these non-citizens subsequently. "Hence the legal Indian citizens lose out against this illegally created citizenry in Assam. This situation is prevalent in states like Meghalaya and Nagaland as well"[78].

Most of the irregular migrants who enter and settle in the state of Assam own very little property in their home country. It is also very difficult for them to acquire land and other assets due to population pressure. In contrast, in the state of Assam, it is relatively easier to acquire land and other properties. The availability of vast public land in Assam has, therefore, attracts millions of Bangladeshis to the State. "The riverine deltas along the river Brahmaputra and other major rivers were mostly uninhabited. Moreover, a large part of the state was covered by forests. The immigrants with little resistance, could, and still can, encroach upon those lands. In recent decades, immigrants not only have encroached lands in reserved belts and blocks for the tribal population in Assam"[79].

Form the above analysis it can be said that, economic factor can act as both pull as well as push factors behind migration of people from Bangladesh to Indian States. It has been observed by many scholars that economic migrants from Bangladesh are the major contributor to the total stock of migrant population in India. Apart from religious persecution, millions of people from both Hindu and Muslim community left Bangladesh and continues to do so due to breakdown of their economic condition and the state's incapacity to repair them in their own country.

**Environment Factors:**

"Now all of them are not coming to India, but it would be not implausible to believe that some of them would be. The inherent law of migration... is that people move to areas close to themselves which are compatible, geographically and culturally. Over a period of time this out flow can cross international borders". Hazarika, 2002, p.27

Several environmental factors in Bangladesh have pushed millions of its population to severe poverty by breaking their source of livelihood and destroying their habitats. Bangladesh's geographical location has made it vulnerable to several environmental hazards like floods, droughts, cyclones, sea level rise and many others. It has faced the worst type of natural calamities in the past. In the recent year the ongoing phenomena of global warming and climate change has made the situation more precarious and it has been predicted by the United Nation Inter Governmental Panel on Climate Change (IPCC) that Bangladesh could lose nearly one fifth of its land by 2050 due to rising sea levels as the global warming is going on[80]. Thus Bangladesh is highly vulnerable to the negative consequences of climate change. It is to be noted that there exist a close relationship between climate change and migration decisions of Bangladeshi people who are migrated to the Indian state of Assam, West Bengal, Delhi, Mumbai, Odisha and many other places.

Many scholars have observed that climate change coupled with environmental depletion in Bangladesh may act as push factor that drive people to move to India[81]. Sarfaraz Alam, a well known scholar argues that the major reason for continued Bangladeshis' migration to India is environmental crisis and its impact on the people of Bangladesh. Alam has interlinked factors like scarcity of natural resources, environmental change and rapid population growth in Bangladesh and their migration decisions[82].

In fact, the natural resources in Bangladesh are not sufficient for its increasing population. Adding to this problem, the serious devastation of climate sensitive source of income due to rapid changes in earth's climate condition has resulted in ecological and economic marginalisation of the poor Bangladeshis. The low economic prospects seems to be a major push factor which forces the affected people to move toward

India where the economic prospects appear to be better[83]. Thus in case of environmental crisis the affected Bangladeshis have two options i.e. either to adapt or to leave the country as their source of income and homes are destroyed.

The International Organisation for Migration (IOM) in 2010 reports that, Bangladeshis are threatened by large ranges of sudden onset of disasters such as storms, earth quakes, tsunamis, and floods. Sea level rise and salt water intrusion are another long term process of natural disasters in Bangladesh[84]. Thus Bangladesh is, at present, considered as one of the most vulnerable countries in the world due to climate change and environmental degradation. The country's 25% of territory is inundated during monsoon and up to 70% is exposed to intermittent extreme flooding[85].

***Geographical Location of Bangladesh:***

Bangladesh is the extremely densely populated country where the population was 142 million in 2005, and it is expected to reach 243 million by 2050[86]. "Therefore extremely densely populated, the country is almost entirely located in a gigantic delta of three rivers: floods plains of Ganges, Brahmaputra, Meghna and smaller rivers occupy about 80 percent of the country; hills occupy 12 percent and uplifted faults blocks (so called terraces) 8 percent: With 230 rivers, of which 57 are international, Bangladesh is in most cases the lower riparian country, and almost 70% of the entire national territory is less than one meter above the sea level"[87].

As Bangladesh is located on the tropic of cancer, it experiences heavy monsoons, and receives significant precipitation between the months of May and September. The intensity of annual rainfall is also vary from places to places with some areas receives heavy rain fall where as some areas receives few. In an average year, 40% of Bangladesh's total land area is flooded with river erosion washes away 1% of arable land[88]. Floods in Bangladesh are generally caused by monsoon rains and are also linked to melting Himalayan glaciers. It is predicted that by 2030, Bangladesh could lose up to 20% of its land[89]. This prediction even got more strength when one consider that Bangladesh's biggest island known as Bhola island was swallowed by rising sea level which left 500,000 people homeless[90].

The 2008 Census Report says that, 88.45 percent of Bangladeshi households are located in rural areas. The Government of Peoples Republic of Bangladesh, 2008 says that though the level of poverty decreased from 59% to 40% between 1991 and 2005, more than 50 million people still live below poverty line and in the most ecologically endangered areas of the territory[91]. Moreover, Bangladeshis are mostly dependent on traditional rice production which occupies about 80% of the cropped areas[92].

### *Environmental Catastrophe in Bangladesh and its Impact upon People*

Tsunamis to water scarcity, caused by its geographical location and due to the present climate change are major environmental problems seriously affecting the economy and development process in Bangladesh. In 1974 heavy storms produced a flood which was again followed by a famine killing 30,000 people[93]. The Tornado of 1989 killed about 1000 in north-west of Dhaka after several month of long drought that destroyed most of the crop[94].

Thus flood affects millions of people in Bangladesh where as storms severely damages both crops and economy in the country. It is the most dangerous disaster which not only affects the security of the people but also their source of livelihood. During the last 30 years, environmental disaster have provoked tragic humanitarian crisis in the country.

The most affected section of people, finding no other option, will definitely decide for internal or external migration. In 2010, the International Organisation for Migration stated that natural disasters will continue to destroy the life and livelihood in the coming days and this destruction will play an important role for Bangladeshis' decisions for migration. It is to be noted that the poor and small land holders are the most affected section due to natural disasters in Bangladesh.

***Linking Environmental Factor and Migration Decision:***

Environmental factor in the form of natural disasters continues to be an important component of people's migration decision in the 21st century. Floods in Bangladesh have always pushed the Bangladeshis to its neighbouring India. The affected people make a departure from all those areas which are less ecologically fragile territories. Thus environmental factors among which floods are the most important one shapes the people decision to migrate. With regard to the number of Bangladeshi people found to be present in India, it is held that, since the independence of the country (Bangladesh) in 1971, approximately 12 million Bangladeshis have illegally migrated to the North-East India[95]. It is held by a scholar that, since the early 2000 the number of these illegal migrants in India is closed to 20 million, though this remains contested by the Bangladeshi government. All these migrants have not only settled in Assam and other North East Indian states but also spread to West Bengal, Delhi, Mumbai and Odisha. Homer-Dixon, 1994, made it clear that, since the end of the Second World War up to 17 million Bangladeshis had moved to India due to environmental problem. The flood-migration nexus clearly says that due to the increasing displacement of rural population they are either migrated to the urban Bangladesh and most importantly to India crossing the international border. Among the countries which are mostly likely to be affected by climate change phenomena, Bangladesh remains in the front line which necessitates the task of devising programmes and policies for a solution to the crisis.

Thus environmental problems like frequent floods, brutal

cyclones, droughts, river bank erosion, water logging etc are the major natural disasters frequently affecting the Bangladeshis. Every year such environmental disaster kills and displaces many people. "About 0.6 million people were killed in Bangladesh in 2011 and 6 million were affected by natural disasters"[96]. In addition to the natural disasters, many man-made calamities have affected the natural environment and economic condition of people there. In this sphere "the Farakka Barrage and also the Katpai Dam, which has displaced around 100,000 people and inundated 54,000 acres of plough land, hence destroying the livelihood of the indigenous people of those areas"[97].

It is to be noted that, although environmental factors play a vital role triggering migration in Bangladesh, it (migration) cannot be taken place in isolation to other factors such as political, economic, social and cultural. Because all these factors can shape or change people's decision for migration. For instance, a flood has its impact upon the agriculture of the people i.e. on the economy and livelihood of the people and consequently shaping migration decisions. Similarly cultural linkage between the people of the destination country and the affected people can be a pull factor behind migration.

***Climate Change and Bangladeshis' Migration:***

"The climate of Bangladesh is already undergoing rapid changes causing displacement of a huge number of people". (UNO's report on World Population Prospects, published in Niyamia Barta, 22, April 2016)

In the recent year the phenomena of global warming and climate change constitutes another serious threat to Bangladesh. These phenomena, thus, add to the ongoing natural calamities which regularly causes devastation in Bangladesh. S.K. Hasina, the Prime Minister of Bangladesh showed serious concern to the problem of global warming in an international conference held in Indonesia. She was of the opinion that global warming will cause the sea level to rise in the next few years, and the consequence will be the submergence of many coastal areas of Bangladesh under water, rendering the areas inhabitable. The Prime Minister again observed that such phenomena will displace more than 30 million Bangladeshis, without adequate rehabilitation space[98]. So the outcome is clear i.e. these people will enter mostly to neighbouring India in search of safer heaven[99]. The Eastern part, being the most accessible areas of Bangladeshi migrants, will be the main destination in India.

James S Pinder, a scholar says that the severity of climate change will surface in Bangladesh, in the following manners "Average weather temperature rising; more extreme hot and cold spells; rainfall being less when it is most needed for agriculture, yet more in the monsoon when it already causes floods; melting of glaciers in the source area of Bangladesh's river altering the hydrological cycle; more powerful tornados and cyclones; and sea level rise displacing communities, turning fresh water saline and facilitating more powerful storm surges. The impact will be intensified by the fact that Bangladesh is both one of the most populated and one of the poorest nations on earth"[100]. Bishop Michael S. Baroi, another scholar stated that "It would be a serious catastrophe for my country and for the whole region if much of the land in Bangladesh disappears under the sea. I become frightened to think that my grand children will have no place to live on this planet earth. I really want to be sure that they, and their children after them, will be able to enjoy the beauty of my country that I have enjoyed, and will be able to have enough land to live and enough land for food"[101]. This view of the scholar clearly reflects the upcoming danger that Bangladesh is going to face due to changes in earth's climate.

Bangladesh's urban areas and capital cities are becoming overcrowded day by day due to population increase and rural to urban migration. There is almost 5 percent growth in the twenty million capital city population of Bangladesh. The rural people in Bangladesh, having lost their homes and livelihoods due to worsening river erosion and storm surges, are migrated to the cities in search of a livelihood. The Vice Chancellor of Independent University, Bangladesh once said that, migration flow from the rural to urban areas will increase as climate change problems like sea level rise intensify[102]. And these will consequently double the city population and in such a situation the people will definitely look towards India for their settlement.

The Assamese daily Niyamia Barta on 12th of May 2016 reported that, under the rising water level, five islands of the Pacific near Solomon have already disappeared and six more islands are likely to face the same consequence in the coming days.

In a nut shell, the ongoing phenomena of global warming and climate change already affected the life and livelihood of millions of Bangladeshis. As rural to urban migration is not a suitable solution to their problem, millions of Bangladeshis continues to see towards India as a place of destination. Thus such changes in the climate condition are an alarm signal, for the Indian states sharing their border with Bangladesh.

**Other Facilitating Pull Factors:**

There are certain pull factors that attracts millions of Bangladeshis towards India. Under this one can include factors like, porous Indo-Bangladesh Border, pre social network, presence of vested interests, political support in the place of destination.

***Porous India-Bangladesh Border:***

The Porous India-Bangladesh border has facilitated the illegal entry of millions of Bangladeshis to the north eastern states of India and West Bengal. These migrants subsequently spill to other Indian cities like Mumbai, Delhi, Gujarat, Odisha etc. The border between India and Bangladesh cover a length of 4,096.76 kilometre. Out of this 4096.76 long India-Bangladesh border 1,116.2 kilometre is riverine and 2979.5

kilometre is land border. Only 719.16 kilometre of riverine border is feasible for erection of fence while remaining 397.04 kilometre is not feasible[103]. Many parts of this border are very porous in nature. The border includes plains, mountains, rivers, wetlands, jungle terrain, agricultural lands, national parks, sanctuaries, reserve forests, large estuaries and enclaves having remarkable biological and environmental diversity[104]. However, in many places the international boundary cuts through rivers, mountains, char lands, agricultural lands and public institutions.

The Porous nature of the border facilitates easy entry of Bangladeshis to India illegally. The riverine borders are particularly used by the infiltrators for illegal entry. It is also very difficult to watch each stretch of the riverine border. The presence of many points along the riverine border which is known as ghats facilitates illegal and easy ingress[105]. The chars formed on the river beds also facilitate illegal entry of the migrants to the Indian mainland[106]. It is to be noted that the north east part of India shares about 2,000 kilometre of Porous border with Bangladesh. Infiltration from Bangladesh generally takes place through the gaps in land border, river border, char islands, forests and hilly terrain[107].

In fact it is not possible to construct boundary pillars throughout the border as it involves many inaccessible areas. Moreover, lack of fencing on the border creates problem in proper patrolling and consequently there takes place illegal infiltration[108]. Hiranya Kumar Bhattacharya in his book 'Illegal Migration from Bangladesh' is of the opinion that, the indifferent attitude of the government of India and the Assam government to maintain strict vigilance and seal the India-Bangladesh border has practically resulted in an invitation to the Bangladeshis to infiltrate[109].

It is reported in the Assam Tribune dated. 25$^{th}$ of February 2016 that, "Nearly 30 percent watch post meant for keeping a tab on illegal infiltrators are laying non functional in the state as the law enforcing agencies continue to remain clueless about 37,789 untraced illegal Bangladeshi immigrants who came to Assam post 1971"[110].

***Pre-Social Network:***

The social network established between the old migrants who entered India earlier and the fresh migrants are particularly very important factor for the illegal entry of people at the border. The old migrants provide various kinds of help to the new migrant i.e. in obtaining "required official documents to settle permanently in India"[111]. Thus the existence of such social network removes the fear psychosis among those Bangladeshis who cherish the intention to enter India due to many compelling factors in their home land. The existence of pre-social network is not a new factor enabling the entry of migrants but its presence can be traced back to the century back.

***Presence of Vested Interests:***

The vested interests within India has been the another facilitating factor enabling infiltration across India-Bangladesh border. There are reports of some Border Security Force (BSF) personnel claiming money from the Bangladeshi migrants to go for other way when these migrants try to cross the India-Bangladesh border[112]. It has also been observed that some of the border guarding forces joined with the smugglers and touts for monetary benefits[113]. It cannot be denied that every tout or smuggler is "assigned specific patches along the border, locally called the ghats, to facilitate border crossing by prospective immigrants and smugglers"[114].

Moreover, these smugglers are locally known as Dalals, who charges money from the prospective migrants for their illegal and clandestine border entry. They also arrange food, shelter and provide employment to them in the destination. A total of Bangladeshi Taka 3,000-5,000 are charged from the migrants caught at the border. What is worst of all these things is that, the money "collected is shared equally among the border-guarding forces of India and Bangladesh and the dalals"[115]. It is to be noted that, not all the border forces of India and Bangladesh are in contact with the smugglers. So it is incorrect to blame the entire security forces due to some ill minded and greedy security forces. There are many instances where the BSF of India has intercepted thousands of Bangladeshis who were trying to infiltrate India illegally.

***Political Support at Destination:***

The favourable internal political situation in India specifically in the north east and the West Bengal has acted as a pull factor behind illegal entry of Bangladeshis to all those states of India. The political support given to the migrants can be traced back to the British rule in India. The Muslim League government of Saadulah at that time not only encouraged thousands of Muslims to come to Assam from East Bengal, but also made all the arrangements for their easy settlement in Assam region. Mr. Saadullah's main objective was to convert Assam into a Muslim majority region so that his hold on the political scenario of Assam will be strengthened.

In the post-independent India power politics continues to influence the political parties to support the irregular Bangladeshi migrants. Even still today it continues to encourage the Bangladeshis to illegally enter India. Millions of irregular Bangladeshis have been converted into Indian citizen only due to the evil political interests of some political parties in the region. Whenever there is any attempt to detect and deport these irregular migrants in Assam, some political parties alleges that the government is trying to harass the Indian Muslims. Many political parties even go against the executive and seriously criticise their action. In the year 2018, when the Government of India published the draft report of National Register of Citizens (NRC), where forty lakhs people were found to be foreigners, then the Trinamool Congress (TMC) government under the leadership of Mamata Banerjee in West Bengal seriously alleged that the central government is harassing the Muslims in Assam. It also threatened the Central government regarding the bad consequences of implementation of the NRC by saying that the government (at the centre) should not play with fire in the name of NRC. The TMC in West Bengal reiterated the claims of the then Jyoti Basu government which stated "that there are no illegal migrants in his state West Bengal."[116]

In fact, some political parties in Assam and West Bengal consider these irregular Bangladeshi migrants as potential vote-banks which could help them to remain in political power. Therefore, these political parties have not only facilitated the illegal entry and stay of Bangladeshi migrants, but also helped them in obtaining fake voter identity cards, ration cards etc. In return these fake Indian citizens also render absolute loyalty to them during the time of election.

There took place significant movement of Bangladeshi migrants, mainly form Muslim community, during the period of few Congress leaders which included Mainool Haq Choudhury, Faqruddin Ali Ahmed, Abdul Ghani Khan Choudhury and Santosh Mohan Dev to some extent[117]. Siddharth Shankar Ray who led a Congress government in West Bengal maintains a passive attitude and remained quite to the migration problem. The CPM government under Jyoti Basu supported the cause of Hindu migrants from Bangladesh and allowed them to settle in West Bengal[118]. The situation was similar in Assam. In fact the Muslim migrants in Assam were both left and right hand of the Muslim leaders of Assam tilting the election results in favour of Congress in 1990s. In 1990, Hiteshswar Saikia had declared in Assam Assembly that there were no single foreigners in Assam[119].

Since 1985, those who became the Chief Minister of Assam made no serious effort to detect and deport the irregular

Bangladeshi migrants from the state. However, when the National Democratic Alliance (NDA) came to power under the Prime Ministership of Mr. Narendra Modi, there have been many attempts to detect the irregular Bangladeshi migrants in the state of Assam. In this sphere, under the supervision of the Supreme Court of India in the year 2018, the NRC published its first draft report where the names of four million people in Assam were missing from the citizens list. The publication of the report created serious resentment by various political parties. Mainly the TMC in West Bengal was against the NRC report. As the report of the NRC was a draft report, the Government of India did not take any action against the migrants because the name of many true Indian citizens was missing from the list. On the 31st August 2019, the final report of the NRC was published where the name of 19.6 lakh[120] people of the state of Assam was missing creating fresh tension in the state. However, no strict action has been taken to deport these migrants as the issue has again been politicised.

Thus all these factors are responsible for the irregular migration of millions of Bangladeshi population to the various states of India.

## References


1. Government of Assam (2012), *White Paper on Foreigners' Issue,* Home and Political Department, October 20, 2012.
2. Bhattacharyya, Hiranya Kumar. (2018), *Operation Lebensraum: Illegal Migration From Bangladesh,* New Delhi: Bloomsbury Publishing India Pvt. Ltd.
3. Mishra, P.K. (2014), *Bangladesh Migrants: A Threat to India,* New Delhi: Gyan Publishing House.
4. *ibid.*, p. 50.
5. Bhattacharyya, Hiranya Kumar. (2018), *Operation Lebensraum: Illegal Migration From Bangladesh,* New Delhi: Bloomsbury Publishing India Pvt. Ltd.

6. Goswami, Uddipana. (2010), "Miya or Axamiya? Migration and Politics of Assimilation in Assam", *Journal of Social and Policy Sciences*, Vol. 1, No. 1, pp. 7-8.
7. Guha, Amalendu. (2006), *Planter Raj to Swaraj: Freedom Struggle & Electoral Politics in Assam 1826-1947*, New Delhi: Tulika Books.
8. Government of Assam (2012), *White Paper on Foreigners' Issue*, no. 1, Home and Political Department, October 20, 2012.
9. Das, Pushpita. (2016), *Illegal Migration from Bangladesh: Deportation, Border Fences and Work Permits*, New Delhi: Institute for Defence Studies and Analyses.
10. Between 1951–61, 1961–71 and 1971–81, the population of India grew from 21.64 per cent to 24.80 per cent to 24.66 per cent. "Size, Growth Rate and Distribution of Population", in *Census of India*, 2011," URL: http://censusindia.gov.in/2011-provresults/ data_files/india/Final_PPT_2011_chapter3.pdf, accessed on January 27, 201.
11. Seventy Third Report of the Committee on Petitions, Rajya Sabha, New Delhi, March 22, 1982, p. 4.
12. Das, Pushpita. (2016), *Illegal Migration from Bangladesh: Deportation, Border Fences and Work Permits*, New Delhi: Institute for Defence Studies and Analyses.
13. Bhaumik, Subir. (1996), *Insurgent Crossfire: Northeast India*, New Delhi: Lancer Publishers.
14. Government of Assam, "Infiltration and Deportation of Pakistanis", Directorate of Information and Public Relations Press Note No. 137, July 27, 1965, Shillong, [Online: web] Accessed 5 February 2015 URL: http://online.assam.gov.in/documents/218410/316853/Annexure-2-17A-except-9- and-12.pdf.
15. Das, Pushpita. (2016), *Illegal Migration from Bangladesh: Deportation, Border Fences and Work Permits*, New Delhi: Institute for Defence Studies and Analyses.
16. Sarma, Madhumita. (2015), *A Study of Migration from Bangladesh to Assam, India and Its Impact*, Ph.D Thesis, Adelaide, SA 5005, Australia: The University of Adelaide.

17. Hazarika, S. (2000), *Rites of Passage, Border Crossing, Imagined Homeland, India's East and Bangladesh*, India: Penguin Books.
18. Bhattacharyya, Hiranya Kumar. (2018), *Operation Lebensraum: Illegal Migration From Bangladesh,* New Delhi: Bloomsbury Publishing India Pvt. Ltd.
19. Sarma, Madhumita. (2015), *A Study of Migration from Bangladesh to Assam, India and Its Impact*, Ph.D Thesis, Adelaide, SA 5005, Australia: The University of Adelaide.
20. *ibid.*, p. 42.
21. *ibid.*, p. 44.
22. Mishra, P.K. (2014), *Bangladesh Migrants: A Threat to India,* New Delhi: Gyan Publishing House.
23. *Ibid.,*
24. Bhattacharyya, Hiranya Kumar. (2018), *Operation Lebensraum: Illegal Migration From Bangladesh,* New Delhi: Bloomsbury Publishing India Pvt. Ltd, p. 31.
25. Mishra, P.K. (2014), *Bangladesh Migrants: A Threat to India,* New Delhi: Gyan Publishing House, p. 67.
26. "Be Right Back: Bangladeshi Deportees Show Stoic Resolve", *The Times of India,* Ahmedabad, January 29, 2013, [Online: web] Accessed 5 February 2017 URL: http://timesofindia.indiatimes.com/city/ahmedabad/Be-right-back-Bangladeshi-deportees show-stoicresolve/articleshow/18230619.cms.
27. "Over 40 K Illegal Bangladeshi Migrants Deported: FRRO to Court", *Business Standard*, New Delhi, August 20, 2013, [Online: web] Accessed 5 January 2018 URL: http://www.business-standard.com/article/pti-stories/over-45k-illegal-bangladeshi-migrants-deported-frro-to-court-113082000822_1.html.
28. "Political Pawns", *India Today*, August 10, 1998, [Online: web] Accessed January 28, 2019 URL: http://indiatoday.intoday.in/story/shiv-sena-bjp-govt-launches-operation-in-mumbai-to-push-illegal-bangladeshiimmigrants- back/1/264716.html .

29. "Nearly 8500 Bangladeshis Living Illegally in Uttar Pradesh", *DNA*, Lucknow, June 11, 2010, [Online: web] Accessed April 23, 2015, URL: http://www.dnaindia.com/india/report-nearly-8500-bangladeshisliving- illegally-in-uttar-pradesh-1395139 .

30. "Bihar: Borderline Cases", *India Today*, July 13, 2012, [Online: web] Accessed April 23, 2015, URL: http://indiatoday.intoday.in/story/now-bihar-sees-agitation-against-illegal immigrants-frombangladesh/1/372111.html.

31. "Government Identifies 3, 987 Bangladeshi Infiltrators in Odisha", *The Economic Times*, Bhubaneswar, March 18, 2013, [Online: web] Accessed April 23, 2017, URL: http://articles.economictimes.indiatimes.com/2013-03 18/news/37814738_1_infiltratorsbangladeshi-nationals-minister-naveenpatnaik.

32. The New Indian Express, 20th January, 2018.

33. *Ibid.,*

34. *Ibid.,*

35. Das, Pushpita. (2016), *Illegal Migration from Bangladesh: Deportation, Border Fences and Work Permits,* New Delhi: Institute for Defence Studies and Analyses.

36. "Internal Note Prepared by the Home Ministry, Government of India, March 1992", in Kumar (ed.), *Illegal Migration from Bangladesh*, n. 11, pp. 243-57.

37. Das, Pushpita. (2016), *Illegal Migration from Bangladesh: Deportation, Border Fences and Work Permits,* New Delhi: Institute for Defence Studies and Analyses.

38. "Lots of Bangla Migrants, How Many We don't Know: Jaiswal", *The Economic Times*, New Delhi, February 20, 2009, [Online: web] accessed on February 28, 2015, URL: http://articles.economictimes.indiatimes.com/2009-0220/news/27638067_1_bangladeshi-infiltrators-illegal-bangladeshi-migrantsborder-districts.

39. "Writ Petition (Civil) No. 125 of 1998, All Indian Lawyers Forum for Civil Liberties (AILFCL) & Another Vs. Union of India and Others, Counter Affidavit on behalf of the Respondent

No. 3", in Kumar (ed.), *Illegal Migration from Bangladesh*, n. 11, pp. 140, 271.

40. Das, Pushpita. (2016), *Illegal Migration from Bangladesh: Deportation, Border Fences and Work Permits,* New Delhi: Institute for Defence Studies and Analyses.

41. Bhattacharyya, Hiranya Kumar. (2018), *Operation Lebensraum: Illegal Migration From Bangladesh,* New Delhi: Bloomsbury Publishing India Pvt. Ltd, p. 35.

42. Grover, Verinder and Arora, Ranjana (1999), *Partition of India: Indo-Pak War and the UNO*, New Delhi: Deep & Deep Publications.

43. Das, Pushpita. (2016), *Illegal Migration from Bangladesh: Deportation, Border Fences and Work Permits,* New Delhi: Institute for Defence Studies and Analyses, p. 28.

44. *ibid.*, p. 28.

45. Guhathakurta. Meghna, (2103), "Amidst the Winds of Change: The Hindu Minority in Bangladesh", in Tanweer Fazal (ed.), *Minority Nationalisms in South Asia*, *South Asian Culture and History*, New York: Routledge.

46. Bhattacharyya, Hiranya Kumar. (2018), *Operation Lebensraum: Illegal Migration From Bangladesh,* New Delhi: Bloomsbury Publishing India Pvt. Ltd, p. 35, p. 24.

47. Mohapatra, Atanu and Sahoo, Prakash Chandra. (2014), "Violence Against Minority Hindus in Bangladesh: An Analysis", [Online: web] Accessed 7 August 2019 URL: https://www.vifindia.org/article/2014/july/30/violence-against-minority-hindus-inbangladesh-an-analysis.

48. Das, Pushpita. (2016), *Illegal Migration from Bangladesh: Deportation, Border Fences and Work Permits,* New Delhi: Institute for Defence Studies and Analyses, p. 30.

49. Mohapatra, Atanu. and Sahoo, Prakash Chandra. (2014), "Violence Against Minority Hindus in Bangladesh: An Analysis", [Online: web] Accessed 7 August 2019 URL: https://www.vifindia.org/article/2014/july/30/violence-against-minority-hindus-inbangladesh-an-analysis.

50. *ibid.*, p. 2.

51. Lintner, "Religious Extremism and Nationalism in Bangladesh", n. 45, p. 416.

52. Bhardwaj, Sanjay. (2014), "Illegal Bangladeshi Migration: Evaluating India-Bangladesh Approaches", *CLAWS Journal, 68.*

53. Das. Bhaswati, & Ansary, Rabiul, (2017), *"Bangladeshi and Inter-state Migrants: Differential Adaptation and Acceptance by the Locals in West Bengal, India",* Springer.

54. Das, Pushpita. (2016), *Illegal Migration from Bangladesh: Deportation, Border Fences and Work Permits,* New Delhi: Institute for Defence Studies and Analyses, p. 29.

55. Barkat, Abdul (2011), "Political Economy of Deprivation of Hindu Minority in Bangladesh: Living with the Vested Property Act", in Abhijit Dasgupta, Masahiko Togawa and Abdul Barkat (eds.), *Minorities and the State: Changing Social and Political Landscape of Bengal,* New Delhi: Sage.

56. *ibid.*, p. 104.

57. Bhardwaj, Sanjay. (2014), "Illegal Bangladeshi Migration: Evaluating India-Bangladesh Approaches", *CLAWS Journal, 68.*

58. "Hindus under Threat" The Daily Star, January 7, 2014, [Online: web] Accessed 5 August, 2019 URL: http://www.thedailystar.net/hindus-under-threat-5781.

59. "Attacks on Minorities" New Age January 11, 2014 [Online: web] Accessed 4 August, 2019 URL: http://www.newagebd.com/detail.php?date=2014-0111&nid=80020#.U7PpTbHAAUB.

60. "Obhoynagar Reminds of 71 Horrors" Dhaka Tribune January 7, 2014[Online: web] Accessed 4 August, 2019 URL: http://www.dhakatribune.com/crime/2014/jan/07/obhoynagar-reminds-%E2%80%9971-horrors .

61. "Hindus again attacked in Bangladesh on false rumours of defaming Muhammad in facebook" Hindu Existence May 7, 2014 Accessed 4 July, 2019 URL: http://hinduexistence.org/category/attack-upon-hindu-buddhists-by-muslims/ .

62. Mohapatra, Atanu and Sahoo, Prakash Chandra. (2014), "Violence Against Minority Hindus in Bangladesh: An Analysis", [Online: web] Accessed 7 August 2019 URL: https://

www.vifindia.org/article/2014/july/30/violence-against-minority-hindus-inbangladesh-an-analysis.

63. *ibid.*, p. 4.
64. *ibid.*, p. 4.
65. Rahman, Md. Hasibur. (2015), "Agricultural Land Use and Land Susceptibility in Bangladesh: An Overview", [Online: web] Accessed August 7 2019 URL: http://globalcommunitywebnet.com/GlobalFiles/agriculturallanduse.pdf .
66. Government of Bangladesh, *Year Book of Agricultural Statistics-2013,* 25th Series, April 2015, Dhaka: Bangladesh Bureau of Statistics, p. 3, [Online: web] Accessed July 5 2019 URL:http://www.bbs.gov.bd/WebTestApplication/userfiles/Image/LatestReports/AgriYearb ok-2013.pdf.
67. Das, Pushpita. (2016), *Illegal Migration from Bangladesh: Deportation, Border Fences and Work Permits,* New Delhi: Institute for Defence Studies and Analyses, p. 32.
68. *ibid.*, p. 32.
69. *ibid.*, p. 33.
70. Government of Bangladesh (2010), *Report on Labour Force Survey 2010,* Bangladesh Bureau of Statistics, Ministry of Planning, Dhaka, August 2011, p. 6.
71. Das, Pushpita. (2016), *Illegal Migration from Bangladesh: Deportation, Border Fences and Work Permits,* New Delhi: Institute for Defence Studies and Analyses, p. 34.
72. Mishra, P.K. (2014), *Bangladesh Migrants: A Threat to India,* New Delhi: Gyan Publishing House, p. 29.
73. *ibid.*, p. 29.
74. Bhattacharyya, Hiranya Kumar. (2018), *Operation Lebensraum: Illegal Migration From Bangladesh,* New Delhi: Bloomsbury Publishing India Pvt. Ltd, p. 35, p. 36.
75. *ibid.*, p. 36.
76. *ibid.*, p. 36.
77. Goswami, Namrata, "*Bangladeshi Illegal Migration into Assam:*

*Issues and Concerns from the Field"*, Institute for Defence Studies and Analyses, New Delhi, p. 5.

78. *ibid.*, p. 5.
79. Nath, Hiranya K and Nath, Suresh Kr. (2011), "Illegal Migration into Assam: Magnitude, Causes, and Economic Consequences" [Online: web] Accessed July 5 2019 URL: file:///C:/Users/Dell/Downloads/Illegal_Migration_into_Assam_Magnitude_Causes_and_%20(3).pdf.
80. Joseph, Jolin and Narendran. Vishnu, (2013), "Neither Here nor There: An Overview of South-South Migration from both sides of the Bangladesh-India Migration Corridor" [Online: web] Accessed June 4 2019 URL: https://www.iss.nl/sites/corporate/files/Rajan-Joseph-Narendran_South_Asia_SS_migration_lit_review_bibly_June2013.pdf.
81. *ibid.*, pp. 16-17.
82. *ibid.*, p. 17.
83. *ibid.*, p. 18.
84. Quencez, Martin, (2011), *"Floods in Bangladesh and Migration to India"*, The State of Environmental Migration, p.57. [Online: web] Accessed January 11 2019 URL: http://labos.ulg.ac.be/hugo/wp-content/uploads/sites/38/2017/11/ The-State-of Environmental-Migration-2011-57-71.pdf.
85. *ibid.*, p. 57.
86. *ibid.*, p. 57.
87. *ibid.*, p. 58.
88. *ibid.*, p. 58
89. Wax, Emily. (2007), "In Flood-Prone Bangladesh, a Future That Floats," *Washington Post*, 27/9/2007.
90. *Ibid.,*
91. International Organization for Migration Report 2010.
92. Brammer, H. (1990), "Floods in Bangladesh: Flood mitigation and Environmental aspects", *The Geographical Journal,* 156(2): 158-165.

93. *Ibid.*, p. 12.
94. *Ibid.*
95. Kumar, Anand, (2011), "Illegal Bangladeshi migration to India: Impact on internal security", *Strategic Analysis,* Vol. 35(1): 106-119.
96. Sarma, Madhumita. (2015), *A Study of Migration from Bangladesh to Assam, India and Its Impact,* Ph.D Thesis, p.98, Adelaide, SA 5005, Australia: The University of Adelaide.
97. *Ibid.*, p. 98.
98. Bhattacharyya, Hiranya Kumar. (2018), *Operation Lebensraum: Illegal Migration From Bangladesh,* New Delhi: Bloomsbury Publishing India Pvt. Ltd, p. 35, p. 26.
99. *ibid.*, p. 26.
100. *ibid.*, p.27.
101. *ibid.*, p. 27.
102. *ibid.*, p. 28.
103. Mishra, P.K. (2014), *Bangladesh Migrants: A Threat to India,* New Delhi: Gyan Publishing House, p.61
104. Bhardwaj, Sanjay. (2014), "Illegal Bangladeshi Migration: Evaluating India-Bangladesh Approaches", *CLAWS Journal, 65.*
105. Das, Pushpita. (2016), *Illegal Migration from Bangladesh: Deportation, Border Fences and Work Permits,* New Delhi: Institute for Defence Studies and Analyses, p. 36.
106. *ibid.*, p. 36.
107. Mishra, P.K. (2014), *Bangladesh Migrants: A Threat to India,* New Delhi: Gyan Publishing House, p.64.
108. Bhardwaj, Sanjay. (2014), "Illegal Bangladeshi Migration: Evaluating India-Bangladesh Approaches", *CLAWS Journal, 66.*
109. Bhattacharyya, Hiranya Kumar. (2018), *Operation Lebensraum: Illegal Migration From Bangladesh,* New Delhi: Bloomsbury Publishing India Pvt. Ltd, p. 35, p.35-36.
110. Assam Tribune, 25th February, 2016.
111. Das, Pushpita. (2016), *Illegal Migration from Bangladesh:*

*Deportation, Border Fences and Work Permits,* New Delhi: Institute for Defence Studies and Analyses, p. 36.

112. *ibid.*, p. 36.
113. *ibid.*, p. 36.
114. Nandy, Chandan. (2005) "Illegal Migration from Bangladesh to India: The Emerging Conflict", *Mellon–MIT Foundation on NGOs and Forced Migration*, November 20, 2005, p. 85.
115. Das, Pushpita. (2016), *Illegal Migration from Bangladesh: Deportation, Border Fences and Work Permits,* New Delhi: Institute for Defence Studies and Analyses, p. 37.
116. Das, Pushpita. (2016), *Illegal Migration from Bangladesh: Deportation, Border Fences and Work Permits,* New Delhi: Institute for Defence Studies and Analyses, p. 38.
117. Mishra, P.K. (2014), *Bangladesh Migrants: A Threat to India,* New Delhi: Gyan Publishing
118. *ibid.*, p. 63.
119. *ibid.*, p. 63.
120. Sambad, 1st September 2019, Sunday, Sambalpur.

# 4

# Impacts of Irregular Bangladeshis' Migration on the Security Domain of India

> "There is a third category who are neither citizens nor refugees, who come for economic reasons or economic opportunities. These are illegal migrants. Their entry is silent invasion in the country to which they move."
>
> (Former Union Minister of India Mr. Arun Jaitley)
>
> "...the silent and invidious demographic invasion of Assam may result in the loss of geo-strategically vital districts of Assam. The influx of these illegal migrants is turning these districts into a Muslim majority region..."
>
> (The Supreme Court observation in the Sarbananda Sonowal vs Union of India, 2005 case)

## Migration from Bangladesh to India: Historical Background

The security discourse of India has undergone considerable changes due to many developments in international relations. Among other challenges to the national security of India, irregular migration from Bangladesh receives wider attention among researchers, policy makers and government officials due to its multiple effects on the internal and external security of India. Irregular migration is not only a security threat but also a threat multiplier which has already been observed in the context of irregular Bangladeshis' migration in the north-east states of India. Migration of people, both from the Hindu and Muslim community, from the present Bangladesh, which was earlier known as East Bengal and then East Pakistan, was noticed during the colonial rule in India. Initially such migration was for economic reason or escaping from economic exploitation by the land lords in the East Bengal. The labour demand in the tea industries developed by the British government in Assam encouraged thousands of East Bengali to enter the Assam region. Later on, the political interests of some political parties encouraged the ongoing phenomenon i.e. to encourage more number of Muslim migrants to Assam so as to make it a Muslim majority region. Thus in the initial phase of migration, the migrants were welcomed and given all supports to permanently reside there.

Time started passing, but migration or population inflow from East Bengal did not stop. The East Bengal became East Pakistan in 1947 and in 1971 it became Bangladesh. Socio-economic, political, religious and environmental compulsions back in their home forced millions of Bangladeshis, both Hindus and the Muslims to cross over the international boundary and to enter India. In the initial period migration from Bangladesh was not much opposed and even in the post independence period of India the Bangladeshi migrants were considered as sons and daughters coming home. However, such a trend of population influx did not stop, rather assumed a serious proportion day by day. As Assam and other North East and West Bengal shares a long border with Bangladesh, these areas were flooded with migrants and their population now crosses 20 millions as per the estimates of some research organisations.

Assam, the eldest of North-East States, has been the major area of destination of the Bangladeshi migrants, a majority of whom have also settled in West Bengal. Resentment to the Bangladeshi migrants found manifestation during the late 1970s in Assam where the local Assamese apprehended crisis of Assamese identity along with pressure on Assam's economy due to the presence of millions of Bangladeshi migrants. Such resentment took the form of conflicts involving attacks and counterattacks and consequently threatening the internal security of Assam and other north-eastern states. Thus, for the first time after 1971, Bangladeshis' migration to India was considered to be a greatest security threat for India. Many stakeholders of the security discussions including the general populace of Assam apprehended serious threat to India's sovereignty and integrity due to continuous influx from Bangladesh. Although, initially the central government at Delhi and the government of Assam decided to remain silent to the problem stating the problem a non-issue, subsequently the central and the state government of Assam changed their position and considered it as a serious security threat to India.

Among the entire North East, Assam is the worst sufferer of the Bangladeshis' infiltration problem. The State has witnessed the emergence of many insurgent groups who not only fight with the migrants, but also threatens for secession from the Indian Union. Bangladeshi migrants, after their illegal entry into the State have not only changed the demography but also put serious stress on the economy, culture and language of Assam. Increasing Muslim population in Assam (as shown in many Census report of India) posses the potentiality to reduce the local Assamese into a minority and thereby making the problem a demographic invasion in Assam. When the migrants cross the international boundary without valid documents, it violates the sovereign rights of India to control its border. Again, the mushrooming of Muslim population in Assam is the pre-planned design of Pakistan's intelligence agency Inter Service Intelligence (ISI) and fundamentalist elements of Bangladesh. Pakistan is still in anger against India who played a vital role in separating East Pakistan which became Bangladesh in 1971. Increasing number of Muslim population in Assam through infiltration will definitely help these anti-India elements in Pakistan and Bangladesh to cause serious internal disturbance in Assam. Their long cherished intention to create greater Islamic Bangladesh or Pakistan is intended to be fulfilled through such demographic invasion of Assam. They think, higher is the number of Muslim population in Assam, greater will be the chance of demanding a separate Muslim state which could be subsequently annexed either with Pakistan or Bangladesh.

In fact, the religious sentiments of the illiterate Bangladeshis, who have already settled in Assam, and whose number crosses over millions, is exploited by numerous fundamentalist groups who have settled madrasas and mosques in the border areas of Assam. The fundamentalists operate within India and find all help from their parents organisations situated at Bangladesh. Many instances are there which confirms such unholy nexus. Some of these madrasas which was set up to impart education to the Muslim population are working as a place to foment communal tension and indoctrination of the Muslim youth. In such institutions the vulnerable youths are motivated to join terrorist outfits and to launch anti-India activities. Motivational speeches are conducted in these madrasas by the fundamentalist leaders who had earlier entered into India clandestinely and became successful in obtaining Indian citizenship with the help of some political parties and corrupt government officials. These leaders divide the people on communal line so that they can be used to achieve their pre-designed objective. As most of the migrants are illiterate and very poor, they are easily motivated and fall in the hands of terrorist organisations. Moreover, drug trafficking; trafficking of women, girl, cattle and other crimes are given effect by some of these irregular Bangladeshi migrants at the India-Bangladesh border.

Keeping in view the dangerous developments in India-Bangladesh border in Assam and other north east states it can safely be said that Bangladeshi migrants in India poses a serious security threat to Assam and other North East states in particular and India in general. The subsequent section of this chapter involves an analysis of the significant socio-economic, political and environmental changes took place in Assam due to irregular

Bangladeshis' migration followed by an analysis of its internal and external security implications for India due to the uncontrolled and irregular population infiltration form Bangladesh.

## Brief Outline of the Problem

The population of Assam has increased to such a big extent that it reminds us the continuous inflow of migrants to the state. Mainly, the Muslim population has registered a serious growth in Assam in comparison to other Indian states. And as such, under the political support most of such migrants have converted themselves to Indian citizen and this can be noticed in the increase number of voters in Assam.

The latest Census report also shows that the Muslim population in India has grown faster than the population of other community. In other words the population of Muslim community increased by 24 percent, where as the national decadal growth is about 18 percent[1]. In Assam the decadal growth of the Muslim population has also increased to a considerable extent which is changing the demographic profile of the state. All these unaccepted developments in Assam clearly illustrates the demographic invasion of Assam by Muslim migrants who continues to enter India illegally form Bangladesh. Increase of Muslim population has created new ground for the growth of religious fundamentalism and communal politics in the state as the fundamentalists are very much interested to realise their hidden intention and at the same time the political parties prioritise their vote bank than the sovereignty and integrity of India. Thus Assam is in serious threat to lose its identity in such a situation.

Illegal infiltration into the State of Assam has its impact upon the neighbouring Nagaland also. In other words these migrants have started entering into the State of Nagaland and are trying to settle there and hence threatening the demography of the State. In 2003, the then Chief Minister of Nagaland, Neiphiu Rio expressed dissatisfaction and accused Assam government of exporting migrants into Nagaland. The Chief Minster said that, we cannot take any action against these migrants because they are in possession of valid documents which they have procured in Assam with the help of political parties or some government officials. The enormous increase of Muslim population in the state of Nagaland is clear from the fact that approximately half of the shops in Kohima and a number of 75 percent in Dimapur of Nagaland remains closed during Muslim religious occasions. So the irregular Bangladeshi Muslim migrants have already dominated the trading sector of the state[2].

The same thing i.e. the domination of the trading sector is also noticed in Assam. Petrica Mukhim, a well known writer, wrote in the *Telegraph* (Kolkata) on the 4th of December, 2003, that "It may not be too long before somebody with the power of numbers (population) demands a Union Territorial status in Dimapur. Its market areas already look like a mini Bangladesh, albeit more lucrative"[3]. This phenomenon reminds us the demand for an 'Autonomous Muslim Council' in lower Assam under the Chairmanship of an Assam Government Corporation[4].

The excessive Muslim population influx necessarily increases the strength of the fundamentalists who dream of establishing separate religious state on their wish. Once a Muslim leader in Assam threatened to drive out the Indians from Dhubri as these areas are gradually overwhelmed by Bangladeshi Muslims. It is, therefore, the biggest threat to the unity and integrity of India in the present day situation. There has been working many minds to overwhelm the Assam and to separate it from India so that it can mix with the proposed Greater Islamic Bangladesh. Many conspiracies are also hatched to include the name of these migrants in the National Register of Citizens (NRC) list.

In fact the Pakistani ISI's game plan is clear from all these developments in Assam in particular and other North East in general. Their main intention is to increase the Muslim population in Assam and North East through illegal infiltration from Bangladesh so that it can take revenge from India for her role in the separation of East Pakistan, the burn of which still exists in their mind. The ISI, DGFI and Islamic fundamentalists share similar vision i.e. 'More the number of Bangladeshi infiltrators, more are the chances of committing subversive and anti India conspiracies', and consequently destabilising the entire North East'[5].

To sum up, Assam and the north east now faces crisis of identity not only in political fields, but also in economic, linguistic and cultural fields. Millions of irregular Muslim migrants are being instigated to demand for making Bengali as their mother tongue. The economic sector is also flooded with the presence of these migrants. So the day may not be far off when they will make demand for declaring Bengali language as one of the state language and a separate Muslim state inside or outside the Indian territory[6].

In order to understand the security implications of irregular Bangladeshis' migration, it is pertinent to analyse all those changes that have been taken place in the socio-economic, political and environmental structures of Assam and other Indian states due to such illegal infiltration.

## Demographic Change in Assam due to Bangladeshi Infiltration

The population of Assam has registered a phenomenal growth which is evident from the increase in number of voters registered by the Election Commission of India. In Assam the Muslim population increased at high rate. In addition, the increase in the number of Muslim villages in Assam also reflects significant changes in the population structure with an increasing Muslim population.

In fact the native people of Assam do not change their habitat unless forced by environmental circumstances and other natural disasters. Within the period 1901 to 2011, thousands of new villages had surfaced in Assam[7] which reflects the serious changes in the demographic structure of Assam. It is to be noted that there are certain other areas mainly in non-cadastral riverine areas which might not have been covered during the census.

The situation in Assam is undergoing such a rapid change in terms of demographic changes that a day will come where we will have no other option but to face the consequences. India got independence from the British rule on 15th of August 1947 with Assam as its integral part. But the changes in the demographic structure of Assam due to irregular population infiltration from Bangladesh have put Assam in a dangerous situation. Assam is yet to get freedom from the fear of being extinct in the hands of Bangladeshi nationals.

The population of India recorded a rise of 254 percent between 1901 and 1991, whereas during the same period, the population of Assam rose by 577.77 percent[8]. Moreover, on the basis of average national growth, Assam's population in 1971 should have been 69,86,697 where as it shot up to 1,46,25152[9]. Shri A.K Roy the Director General of BSF (Border Security Force), had reported the increasing trend of Assam population during 1972 and 2005. He said that, during this period 12 lakhs of Bangladeshis had illegally entered into India but did not return[10]. It is to be noted that the Indian migrants from other states preferred to settle down in urban areas, industrial areas and other centres of commercial activities. Thus there is no reason for excessive migration to Assam or north-east from within India.

If we analyse the pattern of population growth in Assam we can find the increasing trend in the growth of Muslim population and decreasing trend in the growth of Hindu population.

There has been a significant growth in the Muslim population from 1911 to 2011. Till 2011, it has registered a growth of around four times to the growth of population in 1911. However, no Census was being carried out in Assam in 1981 due to Assam movement (1979-1985).

Leaving aside Kamrup and Nalbari districts all the nine districts (total twenty seven districts), of Assam have become Muslim majority districts. Dhubri district accommodates larger Muslim population among all the districts followed by Berpeta which registered a 70.74 per cent growth in 2011. As Dhubri district is situated at the border of East Bengal, the migrants first enter to the area.

Thus the increase in the Muslim population in Assam is mainly because of huge scale trans-border irregular migration of people from Bangladesh. This phenomenon may ultimately result in a demand for secession and merger with Bangladesh. In other words, the dream of Jinnah could be achieved by these irregular migrants who are actively backed up by the fundamentalists and some political parties. So the unrelenting influx of irregular migrants from Bangladesh into Assam is a matter of grave concern as it is changing the demographic pattern of the Indian State. It is a serious "threat to the identity of the Assamese people and to our national security. It threatens to reduce the Assamese people to a minority in their own state"[11].

## Changes in the Economic Structure of Assam and other North East States

Irregular Bangladeshi migrants, both Hindus and Muslims, are instrumental in causing significant changes in the economic spheres of Assam, Nagaland and other Indian states. In the state of Assam the infiltrators provide a cheap source of labour and are engaged in many informal sectors. As they are ready to work with comparatively low prices even in odd hours, no one care for the thousands of unemployed Assamese youths. If the migrants were not there (in Assam) the employer would have no other option but to engage the local youths in work sectors with their desired wages. As these migrants shows readiness to work with minimum wages no body listen to the demands for a better wage. In short it has changed the wage structure in Assam considerably and the consequence is the large scale unemployment in Assam.

The trade sector in Assam and Nagaland has also registered significant changes with the domination of Bangladeshi Muslim migrants. These migrants have established their business centres in parts of Assam and their trade is gradually increasing at a very fast rate dominating the local trade market.

All these developments in Assam remind us the fact of their dominance in a foreign state which has seriously changed the economic structure of the destination country. These changes in the economic spheres of Assam can be summed up under the following points:

**Impoverishing the Country's Economy:**

The activities of the irregular Bangladeshi migrants have serious impact upon the economy of India. In the other words these migrants have been responsible for causing huge outflow of Indian money to Bangladesh. As per a World Bank report, as referred by the Assam Tribune, dated 6th of February 2015, that "Bangladeshi migrants are sending home huge amount of money every year and according to persons who are well versed with economic affairs, such remittances can adversely affect the economy of the country, from where the money is sent out"[12]. In this report of the World Bank it is mentioned that the Bangladeshi migrants sent home fourteen billion dollars in 2013 from foreign countries and India topped the list of these countries with 6.6 billion dollars sent from India[13]. Moreover, this report also disclosed the prevailing fact that these Bangladeshis prefer India the most because of low cost of migration. So drainage of money from India is sure to cause low availability of fund for India's own use.

### Changing the Work Culture of Assamese People:

In Assam it has been observed that, the local people have stopped tilling their agricultural land themselves and instead, has employed the migrants for tilling their agricultural land. In other words the easy going attitude of the local people of Assam has resulted in the decline of their work culture as they are very much interested to hire agricultural labourer from the migrants stock instead of working themselves. The comfort loving nature of the Assamese youth have made them satisfied with raising only one crop during the year where as the migrants raise three crops during a year. As such the agricultural sector is inundated by the Bangladeshi migrants who are cheaply available in the state. However, such a state of condition has seriously changed the healthy work culture among the local Assamese as was happened with the American youths for abundant availability of slave labour. Thus, without realising the fact that the Assamese are helping the Bangladeshi migrants in their stay in Assam, they are much satisfied to hire a labour for their comfort[14].

This trend has also given rise to the decline in the economic growth of Assam. The per capita income of the indigenous people has registered a declining trend since the economic opportunities are being shared by millions of migrants.

### Pressuring the Job Sector:

Most of the migrants are appointed in the informal sectors as labourer. In Assam the migrants labours are found to be engaged in all most all building or construction sites. Even the government agencies engage them in all those construction work due to their easy availability at cheaper rate. In the Oil Refinery situated at Guwahati of Assam, the migrant labourers are being employed in large number by the contractors without verifying their citizenship. In earlier days working labourer were being imported from Bihar, Madhya Pradesh and Odisha in large number which employed a vast section of people from Indian states. But all these working sectors have now been captured or flooded by Bangladeshi migrants threatening the employment opportunities of the Indian people. It is a non-denying fact that these migrants have opened a full-scale labour market and hence ousting the labours coming from other states of India[15]. Thus these migrants have created tremendous pressure on job opportunities which has increased the rate of unemployment amongst the local population.

## Changes in the Political Sphere of Assam: Influencing the Election Result

Vote bank politics in India is very much deep rooted among many political parties. Due to their desire to capture political power and to perpetuate their stay in government many political parties prioritise vote bank instead of national interests of the country. The same thing is noticed among many political parties in Assam who can go to the extent of supporting the migrants flow from Bangladesh to Assam and other Indian states. Despite the directives of the Apex Judiciary of India regarding the remedial measures to check illegal infiltration from Bangladesh, neither the central or state government showed activeness in this regard. Now the irregular migrants have become a potential vote bank for some political parties as a result of which their identification and deportation have been pushed to the cold storage.

In his book '*Bangladesh Migrants: A Threat to India*', the author P.K. Mishra is of the opinion that, in the post independence era the Congress has been the dominant political force both at the Centre and Assam. And this political party is mainly accused of encouraging large scale infiltration for its political gains[16]. Not only the Congress political party but also the political parties, who were in opposition, also supported the irregular Bangladeshi migrants for their vote bank[17]. These political parties are accused of manipulating the migrants from Bangladesh to illegally cross the India-Bangladesh border.

Subsequently they also help them in enrolling their name in the voter list. Within a very few year the Congress in connivance with few of their supporting NGOs had already transformed the Bangladeshi migrants as India's citizens even by passing Rajiv Gandhi-Assam accord[18].

Not only the political parties but also the educated people in cities are to be blamed as these people employ these migrants as domestic helps with low remuneration and thereby helping the migrants in earning their livelihood. The business community in Assam also accepts them as cheap source of labour force. Corrupt government officials, may be in revenue department or in district office helps these migrants in obtaining various identity cards, government land and reserve forests in return of some money given to them as bribe.

Thus the nexus made among the political parties, some self-centric Indian citizens and corrupt government officials in Assam helps millions of Bangladeshi migrants to stay in India as Indian citizen. However, it is against the greater interests of our country. Protection of the integrity and sovereignty of India, protection of the ethnic culture and their security should be of primary importance to all the stake-holders in this sphere.

A large number of Bangladeshi Muslim infiltrators have already entered into Assam and are successful in registering their names in the Electoral Rolls. In some districts of Assam the irregular migrants are strong enough to influence the election results which have resulted in the increase of Muslim MLAs in Assam's Legislative Assembly.

Between 1972 and 1978, there have been taken place large scale infiltration of Muslims into Assam who have registered their name in the electoral rolls and consequently there has been an increase in the Muslim MLAs from the Brahmaputra valley. In 1983, Congress (I) could return 33 Muslim MLAs of whom 25 were from Brahmaputra valley as shown in the above table. 1985 election gives a decreasing trend but it was short lived[19].

It is to be noted that most of the Muslim MLAs returned from Assam valley are not of the indigenous Assamese Muslims, rather very few Muslim MLAs come from indigenous stock.

Moreover, it is predicted that, in the face of uncontrolled population influx into Assam, the Bangladeshis will be in a position to influence the constituencies reserved for SCs and STs People. Thus it would not be wrong to say that the voters of alien origin have seized the Electoral Rolls of Assam.

The Census of 2011 reveals the fact of reducing the Hindu population and a considerable increase in Muslim population in Assam. In the fifty Assembly constituencies out of 126 constituencies in Assam, the voters of migrants stock are going to be a determining factor in deciding the future election result[20]. In the 27 of these 50 constituencies, the indigenous Muslims will never win any election. In the remaining 23 constituencies the fate of the candidates will be decided by migrant voters. And if the situation continues to remain like this then the wining candidates of the fifty constituencies will have significant influence in the formation of the state government in Assam. Thus the political future of Assam is going to be very uncertain in the coming days. The day may not be far off when a leader of migrant Muslims will become the Chief Minister of Assam[21].

## Pressure on the Environment

### Damaging the Forest Cover in Assam:

The search for living place among the Bangladeshi migrants have resulted in the destruction of forest areas and thereby lessening the forest cover in Assam. As the riverine island areas (char areas) is not sufficient to accommodate the increasing number of irregular migrants, the migrants move towards forest and hilly areas. But "such movement has resulted in the denuding the forest and hill areas in large scale and consequently increasing the process of environmental degradation. According to the Forest Survey of India, Assam tops the list in the country in respect of denuding the forest state-wise"[22]. It has been reported by the Dainik Axom, an Assamese daily April 2016, that 20,000 square kilometre of forest have been destroyed since 1991[23]. The report of the Forest Survey of India makes it clear that in between 1991 and 2003; around 12,833 square kilometres of deep forests have disappeared. The same report says that, Assam was left with only 1,684 square kilometres of deep forests by 2003.

The Bangladeshi migrants have not only destroyed the deep forest cover in Assam, but they have also encroached the wild life sanctuaries and Reserve Forests.

**Impact Over the Water Bodies in Assam:**

One can find the presence of a many lakes in the state of Assam which have emerged from the changes of the course of many rivers. According to the official records, there are 3931 such lakes in Assam, although the exact figure crosses more than 4,000[24]. Such water bodies are very much helpful for the locals as these are used for fisheries or pisci-culture. Moreover, these water bodies can be converted into eco-tourism centres but such steps have yet to be taken.

In this context it is important to mention that many water bodies or lakes in Assam are now in danger zone due to the encroachment by the Muslim migrants of Bangladesh. As such the degradation of these natural water bodies are taking place rapidly.

The practice of wet-cultivation as introduced and extended by the migrants have been responsible in sinking the original dimension and depth of the lakes. It is also seriously causing the devastation of bio-diversity and consequently the environment. If the practice of wet cultivation continues with the present rate then the lakes will completely dry up and put for use as paddy fields[25].

### Threatening the Life of the Wild-life in Assam:

The Bangladeshi migrants have not only affected the forest and water resources in Assam, but the wild animals in many sanctuaries in the state are in danger due to their criminal activities. The migrants have extended help to the poachers of the world famous one-horn rhinoceros. Many of them have been arrested for such criminal activities by the Indian security forces. Moreover, it is reported in many cases that the beef and lather industries in the India-Bangladesh border inside Bangladesh are surviving on cattle heads smuggled from India by these Muslim migrants. Bangladeshi migrants along with some corrupt police officers of Assam have also extended helps to the cattle smugglers[26].

### Polluting the Local Environment:

Lack of knowledge on the benefit of a hygienic life-style and living condition among the Bangladeshi migrants is the main reason behind the pollution of the society where they reside. These migrants are unknown about promoting a hygienic living condition; the practice of defecating in the open is still in vogue amongst a large number of people of their society. Thus wherever they move, their habitation is turned into a slum in no time. Their life style is a serious threat to the beauty of Assam which has the distinction of an attractive place for many tourists all over the world. In a nutshell, economically increased pressure on land, reduction in forest cover, occupation of government's land by these irregular Bangladeshi migrants is a serious problem that needs to be dealt with immediately[27].

## Irregular Bangladeshi Migrants: A Threat to India's Internal and External Security

The former Union Minister of India and veteran politician and statesman Mr. Arun Jaitly once observed that, the primary "duty of any responsible government is to defend its border, prevent any trespass and make the life of the country's citizen safe and secure". A refugee may have humanitarian consideration in India as they are fleeing a country due to persecution, but irregular migrants does not have it and hence cannot be allowed in a foreign country like India. At the time of the partition of India in 1947, Assam was also a painful issue for Pakistan. Pakistani leadership at that time wanted to capture Assam and they did not like the fact of Assam become a part of India just like Kashmir. Some pre-1971 migrants who have come to India for reason of persecution but the same are not true of all post-1971 migrants who have illegally entered the country India. These infiltrators are called as irregular migrants who are neither citizen of India, nor refugees, who came for reason of economic opportunities and in many case pre-designed of Pakistan. "These are irregular migrants and their entry is the silent invasion of the country to which they"[28] move. The Times of India on 2nd of August 2018 quoted a veteran BJP leader, who was also the BJP's State President as "Illegal immigrants (Muslim) from Bangladesh are changing our overall demography, socio-economics, youths are moving towards Western Bharat in search of jobs since those illegal migrants are taking our place. But the secular politicians are overlooking all these factors and shouting against NRC".

Kailash Vijayavargia, the BJP General Secretary in his answer to the *Economic Times*, told that "Due to this huge foreign population, our youths were not getting employment. The Bangladeshi infiltrators are thriving on government resources and curtailing the government services and facilities"[29]. Bangladeshi infiltrators have already made their presence in West Bengal, besides Assam. Mr. Vijayavargia said that "according to our estimates, there would be more than 10 million Bangladeshi Muslims living in Bengal. The consequences are for us to see. Bengal is the conduit for terror funding". Terming Malda district of West Bengal he again observed that, "The Reserve Bank of India (RBI) figures about Fake Indian Currency Notes (FICN).... the maximum number of FICN was circulated from Bengal. Maximum number of rackets was identified in the state and all sorts of illegal movements are also traced here"[30].

The absconding Gorkha Janmukti Morcha leader Bimal Gauranga, reacting on the possible move of the central government to settle the Bangladeshi infiltrators in the Gorkha hill, after the draft NRC was published in August 2018, released a press communication from an unknown location in August 2018 and stated that "I have been made aware of the fact that the state government is secretly measuring lands in our hills. If this is done to settle illegal Bangladeshis from Assam, then it creates national security threat as the chicken's neck region connects the Indian mainland with the northeast and is highly sensitive". He even threatened of severe resentment if any such move is undertaken by the central and the state government[31].

Irregular migration from Bangladesh is, in fact, a matter of grave concern for India as it has altered and continues to do so the social, economic, political and most important the environmental structure of Assam and many North East states. A study conducted by some scholars of Toronto University and the American Academy of Arts and Science, confirms that, fifteen million Bangladeshi nationals have already infiltrated into India. Similarly, The Advancement of Science, another American organisation, in its study stated that twenty millions Bangladeshi nationals are presently staying illegally in India[32]. The presence of such a huge number of foreign populations in Assam and other Indian states is bound to result in destabilising consequences for the country.

In India, the Bangladeshi migrants constitute a biggest threat or danger to both the dimensions of national security of the country. In other words, the internal and external security of India is in danger due to illegal influx of people from Bangladesh. The Supreme Court of India has cautioned the central government about the security threat India is facing due to uncontrolled population inflow from Bangladesh. Every day hundreds of Bangladeshis make their fraudulent entry to Indian states through the long India-Bangladesh porous border and thereby increasing their numbers which crosses 20 millions now. Thus understanding the security implications of these migrants for India is the need of the hour. In other words, securitization of irregular Bangladeshi migration, raising above its mere politicisation, is to be done for the greater interest of India. The nature and intensity of the problem is such that, immediate measures need to be taken before it overwhelm us leaving with no other option but to bend before it.

## Views of Eminent Persons on the Security Implications of Irregular Bangladeshis' Migration

Serious concerns have been expressed by many intellectuals, policy makers, government officials and many others regarding the destabilising impact of irregular migration from Bangladesh over the safety and security of India. Late Gaurishankar Bhattacharya, a most celebrated intellectual and political and literary luminary of Assam who was the leader of opposition in Assam Legislative Assembly for a very long time and also the president of the Assam unit of the Janta Party during the post-Emergency period, once wrote that "Foreign infiltration is the biggest problem of Assam today. It has impaired the political, economic and demographic balance of the State and has made a planned development of the State almost impossible. With the passage of time, it is becoming a growing menace endangering the very existence of the State of Assam and the integrity and safety of India"[33].

Similar and related view point was expressed by another well known intellectual from Punjab known as Balaji Rao. He once wrote "Assam is on fire and will continue to burn till it is reduced to cinders and Bangladeshi Muslims hijack the State. Thanks to the policy of the British rulers for setting unwholesome precedents and Indian leadership, both state and central, which adamantly refuses to see ground realities[34]. Mr. Rao alleges that the British government is responsible for the current problem Assam is facing. Although the British encouraged the movement of people from the then East Bengal to Assam for tea industries and for other economic activities they might not have thought that the problem would subsequently assume a security threat for India. The subsequent Muslim political parties took full opportunity of the prevailing flow of the people to Assam. It provided these parties opportunities to gain political mileage.

Dr. Rajendra Prasad in 1944, who became the first President of the Republic of India, had expressed his dissatisfaction over the unabated infiltration of Muslims into Assam form East Bengal.

Another well known national figure Dr. Birendra Kumar Bhattacharya, a Janapeeth awardee, who subsequently became the President of Sahitya Academy, once observed that 'the politics of land grabbing in Assam is ostensibly expressed in minority politics, which means an issue of land and jobs for Bengali Muslims and Hindu irrespective of their nationality. In reality, as the historical experience shows, it gives rise to a different kind of politics, the politics of demographic expansion and gradually converting it into a politics of language, culture and finally of executive power'[35]. He further quoted a veteran freedom fighter and journalist Harendra Barua as follows: "In the present Census of 1971, out of nearly 15 million people of the State, over four millions, both Hindus and Muslims, were Bangladeshis. Hindus and Muslims are poised almost equally. In 1980 in an estimated population of 18 million, there number is estimated to be eight million. Assam today is faced with the twin problems being either greater West Bengal or prospective Bangladesh. If this trend continues, sooner or later Assam may meet the fate of Tripura or Sikkim"[36].

In his work titled as '*Imperilled Frontiers: India's North-East Borderland*', Nari Rustomji observed that "The hopes and aspiration of the Assamese that they could absorb the hill districts of Assam within their own cultural stream were doomed from the very outset. The Assamese did not realise that people, however primitive, resent the imposition of alien culture. And so, one by one, the hill districts broke away from the parent state. The Assamese have since found themselves in their turn faced with the threat from cultural annihilation. Year after year, immigrants from Bangladesh have been infiltrating into Assam and getting themselves in the host state. But in getting themselves so absorbed, they have clung tenaciously to their own culture and made no attempt to assimilate with Assamese. The Assamese have a legitimate fear that if the influx continues the time will be not far when they will be reduced to minority in their own state and lose their cultural identity"[37.]

The nature and intensity of the problem of irregular migration of people from Bangladesh to Assam is clearly reflected in a letter written by the then Governor General of Assam, Lt. General S.K. Sinha. In his letter to the then President of India, with copies to the Prime Minister and the Chief Minister of Assam, the Governor expressed serious concern to the problem of illegal migration to the state of Assam. He has once more written in The Assam Tribune of the 3rd of June 2016 on 'Tackling illegal migrants issue in Assam'. Some of the important quotations from the article are as follows: "In 1997, the Prime Minister I K Gujural sent me as the Governor of Assam when insurgency and violence were at its peak in the state. I found that the root cause of the alienation of the people of Assam was the illegal migration from Bangladesh changing the demography of Assam with all its adverse political and economic impact. In 1998, illegal migrant voters were in a majority or near majority in 40 of the 126 Assembly constituencies in Assam. Their presence has increased in the last 18 years". He further writes that "Illegal Migration Detection by Tribunal (IMDT) Act ostensible to check illegal migration was actually designed to facilitate infiltration into Assam". He also alleges that 'All the 14 Congress MPs from Assam interfering in political matters'. He goes on to point out that "To this day, hardly anything has been done to implement the recommendations in my report to the President submitted in 1998.... Tarun Gogoi as the Chief Minister maintained that illegal migration was a non-issue"[38].

The views of the Governor S.K. Sinha clearly reminds the fact that political support to the migrants in Assam is a stumbling block to check further infiltration and to save Assam from its identity crisis in language, culture and economy.

Many intellectuals observes that central government's passive attitude to the problem has generated the feeling of alienation among the indigenous people of the north east states of India. And such feeling of alienation gives rise to the demand for a separate state outside Indian union i.e. secessionism. The younger generation in Assam is much disturbed over the issue of Bangladeshi infiltration into Assam and hence they involved in several years of agitation and protests. Such a state of affairs is highlighted by Myron Weiner in his 'Sons of the Soil', that "The Assamese often think of themselves as forgotten and neglected state, within the Indian Union and as neglected people in danger of being overwhelmed by migrants peoples and absorbed by neighbouring state".

Rajmohan Gandhi, a journalist of very high repute and grandson of Mahatma Gandhi once observed "The rest of India does not see us. If seen, we are not recognised. If recognised, we are not remembered. And we are not heard. This has been the charge of the citizens of the north-east against the India majority"[39].

All these intellectuals have unanimously accepted the security threat that India is facing due to irregular and uncontrolled migration from neighbouring Bangladesh. The problem still persists and has even assumed new dimensions with the emergence of tripartite nexus between Migrants-Fundamentalists-Terrorist networks. Moreover, the lack active action on the part of the Central Government of India, (not to mention the role of the NDA government which started the process of NRC in Assam in 2018 and 2019), has created the feeling of alienation among the general populace of Assam. The youths of Assam have started losing their belief on the central government and have also smelled post-motherly attitude to their causes. And as such the demand for secession from the Indian Union is mushrooming. Thus it is high time to think for the cause of the Assamese people, their long standing demand to save Assam's identity need to be addressed with full political will. Mere tokenism is not going to solve the problem rather it will give further scope to the anti-Indians to divide India, by separating Assam from the Indian Union. Thus it is in the greater interest of the country that political party and other stake holders should raise above vote-bank politics and need to cultivate unanimity on the issue to check the demographic invasion of Indian state of Assam.

## Supreme Court's Concern over the Problem of Irregular Bangladeshi Migration

In 2001, the Supreme Court of India expressed concern about the security threat which India is facing due to the presence of undocumented Bangladeshi migrants in India. The Court held that these migrants may pose serious threat to the financial system and other security of the country. The Supreme Court's decision came out in the hearing of a petition filed by an eminent lawyer O.P. Saxena. The Bench, consisted of the Chief Justice and two Judges of the Apex Judiciary observed that, "Bangladeshi migrants were eating into the economy of the country and had to a large extent become a security threat". The lawyer O.P. Saxena alleges that over one crore or ten million Bangladeshi migrants, who had illegally crossed over to India are causing severe strain on the resources of North-

Eastern states and West Bengal. The Bench of the Supreme Court criticised the Government of India "for being passive to resolve the issue and recommended that the government should take steps to tackle the problem, including the deportation" [40] of irregular migrants.

## Irregular Bangladeshi Migration: Process of its Securitization in India

"When migration is said to be securitised, it means that migration is identified as an existential threat which requires emergency measures by the state. As a result the states pursue policies that aim at alleviating the ills arising out of migration. In the context of India, migration from Bangladesh is presented as a security threat. Here the referent States are Assam, West Bengal and the North-East as a whole"[41]. For the Indian sates the security implications of large scale migration from Bangladesh covers areas like demographic change, growth of radicalism, particularly Islamic fundamentalism, regionalism and more important involvement and encroachment of foreign powers on the country' sovereign space[42].

Securitizing an issue involves the task of presenting an issue as an existential threat which requires emergency measures and justifying actions outside the normal bounds of the political procedure. So it legitimises extraordinary measures to deal with the existential threat. It is not that only the state can politicise or securitize an issue, but the social groups can also generate public opinion to securitize an issue.

In the context of irregular "migration from Bangladesh into India, the issue underwent a gradual process of transformation from politicisation to securitization over a span of decades"[43]. Initially migration from Bangladesh (earlier East Pakistan) was welcomed as it was seen as part of home coming. The post independence era, 1947, witnessed a migration of around 14 million Hindus across the border. It was a population exchange where large "number of Hindus migrated from East Pakistan to the border states of West Bengal, Assam, Meghalaya and Tripura in the first decade after"[44] independence.

Subsequently, migration into Indian states was not stopped and millions of people from East Pakistan started pouring into these Indian states. The outcome of such population influx was the emergence of contest involving the locals and the migrants over land and other scare resources. So the prevailing consideration "son and daughters of the nation are coming home" was replaced with hostility and apprehension against the migrants. In Assam, as the ethnic and religious composition of the migrants did not match with that of the local people it created a stressed environment. However, the government machinery at the centre and state level differed in their views on illegal migration. In the other words initially the state government in Assam decided to place restriction over the unlawful movement of the people at the border sharing with East Pakistan in Assam, where as the central government held the view that due to such restriction the Hindus in East Pakistan would be in disadvantageous position[45].

The Assam Pradesh Committee in 1962 passed a resolution which stated that "infiltration of Pakistani nationals without valid travel documents into Assam is likely to endanger the security of the country"[46]. Just before one year, the population as per Census of 1961 revealed that a huge number of people from East Pakistan, mainly Muslims, had made their entry to Assam illegally. Thus the local political and other leaders of Assam started understanding irregular migration of people from East Pakistan as a threat to their society which needs emergency action.

The worsening of relationships with the Pakistani government in the 1960s compelled the Indian counterpart to solidify its stand on migration of people from East Pakistan. And as such, the outcome was a very big drives against irregular migrants which was launched by the government of Assam on central government's direction.

The issue of Bangladeshi migration to India was fully securitized when the AASU and the AGSP started a state wide agitation against illegal Bangladeshi infiltration into Assam. The AASU and AGSP made it clear that irregular Bangladeshi migrants are an existential threat to the identity of Assam, its culture and economic wellbeing. The issue was finally securitized when the Assamese masses overwhelmingly demanded for emergency measures to prevent the illegal entry of Bangladeshi migrants into the state of Assam.

## Emergence of the Hindu Right Political Parties and the Securitization of Bangladeshis' Migration

With the emergence of Hindu nationalism and Hindu right political parties the anti-foreigner issue moved from the border state of North East to the national politics during the last part of 1980s. The political parties and other groups supporting the rights of Hindu people tried to cultivate a deep influence on the Hindu community by espousing the cause of Hindu people in the North East. The Bharatiya Janata Party (BJP), Rashtriya Swayamsevak Sangh (RSS) and Viswa Hindu Parishad (VHP) are important groups supporting the cause of Hindu people. In this sphere threat to the Hindu Rashtra were identified due to the silent demographic invasion by the Bangladeshi nationals in the north east. Thus the BJP and its allies tried to mobilise the Hindu votes by stating their stand against the irregular migration from Bangladesh. In this way the Hindu right political parties and other groups were successful in presenting irregular migration from Bangladesh as a threat to national security[47].

Due to the continuous pressure of the BJP and its allies, the union government undertook certain emergency and extra ordinary measures to check unauthorised infiltration. The

Narshimha Rao government at that time devised an "Action Plan" for identification, detection and deportation of irregular Bangladeshi migrants from India. Although the central government showed its hesitation to implement the plan, the BJP-led state government in Delhi and Maharashtra implemented the action plan by launching special drive in the early 1990s to detect and deport Bangladeshi infiltrators.

Later on the idiom of demographic invasion from Bangladesh became an influential factor which compelled the government at the centre and few state governments to change their earlier stands on the issue of irregular migration. P.M. Syed, the then Union Minister of State, stated in the House of the People in August 1995 that, "there has been continuous influx of Bangladeshi nationals into India for a variety of reasons, including religious and economic consideration. The demographic composition of the border areas have been altered with the new entrants flooding the areas and the local migrating into the interior"[48]. The Government of West Bengal, which had earlier denied any unlawful migration of people to the state, later on agreed the fact of large scale Bangladeshi migration to West Bengal under intense pressure from the local people.

Now the judiciary and the government officials started accepting that irregular migration pose a serious threat to internal and external security of India. The then Governor of Assam S.K. Sinha once observed that due to the large scale migration from Bangladesh the indigenous people in Assam are being reduced to minority. He also added that political, cultural and economic survival of the local Assamese are being jeopardised in such situation. He also warned that increasing Muslim population in the border belt of Assam due to such migration from Bangladesh would result in loose of border areas of Assam to Bangladesh. And in this sphere the Islamic Fundamentalism would be the driving or forceful factor[49]. Again, the Group of Ministers Report of 2001 declared that due to huge unlawful migration from Bangladesh, "demographic changes have been brought about in the border belt of West Bengal, several districts of Bihar, Assam, Tripura and Meghalaya"[50]. The same report further states that "the massive illegal migration poses a grave danger to our security, social harmony and economic well-being"[51].

Thus keeping in view the unaccepted developments in Assam and other north eastern states it can safely be said that, irregular migration from Bangladesh poses a serious threat to the integrity and security of India. In other words the security ramification of this migration can be understood in both internal and external dimensions. Competition over resources, encroaching government land, changing the wage structure, flooding the low skill and semi skill job sectors and thereby depriving the locals from their due has caused serious resentment against the migrants. Such resentment has ultimately taken the form of conflict even violent action and retaliation which have consequently created serious law and order problem and jeopardising the internal peace and security in Assam. The demographic invasion of Assam by the Bangladeshi Muslim migrants has serious destabilising consequences for the sovereignty and integrity of India. In other words the hidden intention of Pakistan's intelligence agency ISI and the fundamentalists of Bangladesh to create Greater Islamic Pakistan or Bangladesh are to be seriously analysed. Their modus operandi are, increase the Muslim population through infiltration in the north east, spread religious antagonism among the Muslim against the Indian state and create serious law and order problem either through communal activities or terrorist activities in the north east in order to realise their objective. Thus irregular Bangladeshi migration is a major security threat which the country India is facing today.

Today the Government of India is devoting much energies and resources, and is also undertaking many measures to check the migration problem. In this connection it is to be noted that, no doubt the government's effort are serious steps to control the problem, but efforts must be undertaken by the general people, industrialists and other stake holders to stop the infiltration from Bangladesh.

## Religious Fundamentalism and Terrorism in Assam and West Bengal

The fundamentalists in Assam always want to maintain their supremacy at the cost of national interests. Even political party like Congress (I) members in order to get the support of the increasing Muslim population adopted communal approach in the infamous election held in 1983. Abdul Ghani Khan Choudhury, a Congress (I) leader from West Bengal once said, 'If Hindu kills one Muslim then Muslims should retaliate by killing three Hindus and the government would support you'. Thus it is clear that the fundamentalists in Assam and West Bengal support the infiltration of Bangladeshi Muslims into the state of Assam, West Bengal and other North East states to further their political interests. However, such communal approach is against the sovereignty and integrity of India because their hidden intention can be summed as: 'Open demand for an autonomous area for Muslims in lower Assam, Threat to drive out the Assamese from the district of lower Assam and demand for making 'Lungi' and 'Topi' the National attire of Assam'[52].

The fundamentalists in Assam get political support from different political parties, which not only encourage them (the fundamentalists) to adopt anti-Indian approach but also allow them to materialise such approach. Mahibul Haque a man known for his anti-India activities in Assam once staged a 'dharna' at Dhubri, soughing anti-India slogan. Even he along with his supporters threatened to drive out the Indians from Dhubri district. In spite of such act he is yet to be arrested, no investigation has been done and Mahibul continues to thrive under political patronage in Dispur[53].

Thus the presence of such anti-India elements and the political support extended to them for vote-bank is essentially a serious threat to the national security of India.

It is to be noted that, there are around 700 Qaumi madrasas who are involved in the task of supporting and training Islamic militants. These militants manufacturing plants function under three parents organisations– Darul Ulum madrasas in Chitagong Lakhan Bazar, Darul Ulum Mounul Madrasas in Hathazari and Jamiatul Islamia Jamia Madrasas in Patiya. These parental madrasas coordinates and produce thousands of Islamic militants. It is also reported that the militants produced form these madrasas are able to contact with the Taliban and Harkatul Jihad groups. Thus these militant organisations which have their base in Bangladesh are operating in Assam. These groups are also very much supportive to the insurgent outfits form North East like the ULFA, MULTA, and NDFD amidst others and help these organisations in creating disturbances in the Assam region. The blast of 30th October 2008 is the example of such unholy collaboration[54].

It is a matter of serious national security concern for India that all these Jihadi groups try to influence the Bangladeshi migrants and involve them in anti-India activities. The 'Jamatul Muzahidin, Bangladesh' (JMB) had set up its camps in the areas inhabited by the Bangladeshi Muslim migrants. These organisations took full advantage of the religious fanaticisms of the illiterate section of the Muslim migrants. Thus many irregular Muslim migrants are being influenced to enrol them in such militants groups to cause subversive activities against India. These recruits are subsequently used to cause terror activities in Assam and other parts of India. The name of Idris Ali and Shahanur Alam are case in point in this regard to cause communal violence in Indian states.

The leaders of such Jihadi organisation try to harbour close relationship with the Muslim migrants stock in Assam so as to increase their terror activities. When the NIA (National Investigating Agency) of India investigated a prominent leader of JMB named Zahidulla, he confessed of purchasing land in village Bhaktardaba of Barpeta district and even marrying of a local girl in order to cultivate close relationship with villagers of migrants stock[55]. Moreover, in his investigation Zahidulla confessed that he has indoctrinated a number of local youths for getting actively involved in Jihadis activities or terror activities. It is an underlying fact that such a leader must have got political and governmental support in Assam otherwise how it would have been possible for him to acquire immovable property in Assam. But no action has been taken by all those officials who helped Zahidulla in obtaining such property without asserting his citizenship status. The thing is going to worsen day by day as the Assam Tribune of 2nd, May, 2016 reported that, the Jihadis have established contacts with the gun runners of Nagaland and Myanmar for acquiring modern weapons[56].

The irregular Bangladeshi migrants are mostly illiterate and are vulnerable to fall victim of religious bigotry. The Jihadis and some political parties try to foment communal tensions with the intention to separate them from other communities mainly the Hindus. However, it not only creates sufferings for the rivals but also thousands of innocent Muslim migrants face untold sufferings.

In fact, the Hasina government in Bangladesh is adopting tough policies which may slow down the progress of Jihadi activities in that country, but Assam will still stand to suffer in the face of unabated infiltration because the fundamentalist seeds have already been sown in the minds of millions of Muslim populations. Thus the evidence suggests that, religious fundamentalism emerged as a biggest threat not only to the existence of Assam but also the security and sovereignty of the Nation.

In 12th October 2014, it was unearthed by the reporter of an Assamese daily *Amar Axom* that, the fundamentalist outfits of Bangladesh are helping the local fundamentalist organisations in Assam in their anti-national activities. Certain educational institutions have been set up where the uneducated Muslim youths are enrolled as students. However, in reality these youths are indoctrinated and are motivated to join terrorist outfits[57]. The bordering districts like Dhubri and Kokrajhar which borders Bangladesh are prone to all such operations. In these bordering districts the youths are motivated to join terrorist group and to indulge in anti-India activities. Religious sentiments of these youths are exploited and in the name of Islam they are indoctrinated and are converted as jehadis. The arrests of some terrorists in the areas confirm the entire facts. It has also been disclosed that these terror blocks are receiving funds and arms form countries like Afghanistan, Pakistan, Bangladesh, Iraq amidst others. The situation in the border district of Assam has been so much blurred that, many innocent Indian Muslim youths are being eyed with suspicion, which foments communal tensions and the government is criticised of harassing the Muslims of the country.

## Religious Fundamentalism and Irregular Migration Threatens the Unity and Integrity of India

In these days it has been observed that millions of Bangladeshis have illegally entered and settled in the North East and West Bengal and the political parties are very much interested to support them in their settlements for mere vote-bank. Pamela Geller the author of a famous article 'Greater Islamic Bangladesh is a serious threat to Indian Integrity, Sovereignty and Hindu majority' once observed that, the Inter Service Intelligence (ISI) of Pakistan and Director General of Foreign Intelligence (DGFI) of Bangladesh are trying to build a Greater Islamic Bangladesh which would include whole of present Bangladesh, West Bengal, Assam, Tripura, Meghalaya and parts of Bihar, Jharkhand and Odisha[58]. The National Investigating Agency of India (NIA) has revealed that a big conspiracy against the sovereignty and integrity of India is being carried out in different parts like Burdwan, Murshidabad, Birbhum, Nadia, Jalpaiguri and in different madrasas stretched out in the border areas of West Bengal. It is to be noted that the poor and illiterate migrants in Assam, West Bengal and other north-east are easily motivated and indoctrinated. When their population in all those areas of North East increases there will be every opportunity for them to demand for Greater Islamic Bangladesh.

Thus Assam is now under serious threat of losing her identity as a region, which is going to be overwhelmed by millions of Muslim migrants from Bangladesh. The government of the state has also not taken any concrete steps to win the confidence of the local Assamese people. No doubt, the All Assam Student Union (AASU) and the Assam Jatiyatabadi Yuba Chhatra Parishad (AJYCP), a student union of India, are to some extent involved in some action to protect the Assamese identity. Even no new leadership has yet emerged to stave off the identity crisis of Assam and their indigenous people. Thus the failure or the unwillingness on the part of the successive Central Government and State Government to adopt effective measures against trans-border illegal migration intensify the fear of being overwhelmed and finally extinct. And as such, infiltration is perpetuated and even occupies more alarming dimensions with heavy population influx and consequently encroachment of more land and more jobs in Assam[59].

## Vote Bank Politics and National Sovereignty

Bharat Verma, the Editor of 'Indian Defence Review' in an editorial issue said that, vote-bank politics has facilitated irregular migration from Bangladesh in the past two decades. He added that, many border districts of Assam are flooded with migrants coming from Bangladesh. In the near future such a situation will be helpful for creating internal upheaval in the country as it is noticed in the case of Kashmir valley now. Mr

Verma said that such a pre planned operation is aimed at separation of Assam from the rest of India. As the neighbouring country like Pakistan and some anti-India elements in Bangladesh cannot go with direct conflict with India for capturing Assam they usually resorts to indirect strategy of communal division and capture of Assam; what cannot be achieved by conventional military wars, can be achieved through infiltration and subsequently internal subversion. They call it jihad[60].

## Bangladeshi Migrants and Their Involvement in Terrorist Network and Drugs Trafficking in India

Bangladeshi migrants have made their entry into the states like Manipur, Nagaland, Meghalaya, Sikkim, Delhi, Rajasthan, Bombay, Pune, Hyderabad, Madhya Pradesh, Uttar Pradesh, Bihar and Odisha. It has been reported by the security agency of India that there are some cases when these migrants are caught for giving shelter to Bangladeshi militant groups and their Huji leader, Jamati leaders, the ISI linkmen, the Laskar-e-Toiba, Harkat-ul-Aansar and many others. These few people also act as link between the DGFI, the ISI and the Indian Mujahideen. In most of the cases it has been seen that for earning easy money these migrants are involved in drug trafficking form Bangladesh, Nepal and Myanmar to India[61]. In his book '*Bangladesh Migrants: A Threat to India*', the author Mr. P.K. Mishra, who also discharged his duties as the Additional Director General in Indian Paramilitary force and subsequently acted as DIG, BSF Nagaland and Manipur and then IG Border Security Force Shillong, has expressed his personal experiences which gives a clear picture on how these Bangladeshi migrants are involved in drugs trafficking. He wrote "I well remember a case in which I was travelling on foot from Balurghat Hilly Road to Klamati Border outpost in North Dinajpur district where the IB is about seven to eight kilometres from the road ahead. I found a person coming in a hilly Balurghat road. On being stopped by us, he gave his address as Balurghat but it was quite clear that he was from Bangladesh. To my utter surprise, when I opened the plastic bag in his career, I found seven kgs of opium in that. It was a case in the year of 1973, and in all probability, the drug smuggling must have been continuing from all these border areas even till now"[62].

India's former Army Chief Bipin Rawat expressed his concern on the danger of irregular Bangladeshi migrants in India. In a statement he said that unlawful Bangladeshi migration poses national security threat to India. In the year 2017 the Intelligence Agencies of India arrested some terrorists who belonged to Bangladeshi migrant stock and played an important role in various terrorist activities in India in conjunction with ISI. To be more specific, the Burdwan blasts in India make it clear that General Rawat's concerns are not baseless[63].

The arrests of a Bangladeshi national S.M. Alam in January 2008 by the Assam police made it clear about ISI's plan to convert north east into a volatile region. Although these irregular migrants are not involved in terrorism in a big way but are involved in gun running, drug running and running of fake currency rackets[64].

## Irregular Migration and its Link to Internal Security in Assam

In 1995 Prof. Ashok Swain, made a visit to the Bengalipura area of Mumbai. Interviews with the local residents confirmed the presence of about 50,000 Bangladeshi migrants in the slum areas. It was also unearthed that Bangladeshi migrants in the locality have started organising themselves to counter discrimination and possible deportation and the situation may lead to violent conflict in the near future[65].

Bangladeshi migrants have also penetrated into the National Capital of India, Delhi. In 1993, in his interview with the migrants at the place Prof. Ashok Swain found that 1,00,000 Bangladeshi Muslim migrants were living in slum colonies near Yamuna river in Delhi. Swain interviewed six Muslim migrants in their slums in Delhi who were very apprehensive of their future. All had come to Delhi in 1980s from the south-western part of Bangladesh, four due to lose of agriculture and two due to river bank erosion. They also admitted the fact of organising them into group so as to avert any threat to their existence in the areas. The security ramification of irregular Bangladeshi migrants once again received wider attention when the senior officials of Central Reserve Police Force and the Indian Army alleged that Pakistan Intelligence is successful in recruiting agents from among the irregular Bangladeshi to create disturbances in the North-East[66].

The Hindustan Times (New Delhi), 20th December 1992 reported that at the time of post Ayodhya communal violence in India in December 1992 in the Nagaon district of Assam the Muslim migrants under the AMLA were strong enough to engineer a brutal massacre evidently to drive out Hindus from their land. Most of these migrants are settled in Nagaon, Darrang, Barpeta and Kamrup districts in close proximity to each other and are organised against threats from the native community.

"Summing up the impact, the Supreme Court of India in the Sabananda Sonowal vs. Union of India case pointed out that... the presence of such large number of illegal migrants from Bangladesh, which runs into millions, is in fact an 'aggression' on the State of Assam and has also contributed significantly in causing serious 'internal disturbances' in the shape of insurgency of alarming proportion making the life of the people of Assam wholly insecure and the panic generated thereby has created a fear psychosis... The impact is such that it not only affects the state of Assam but it also affects its sister state like Arunachal Pradesh, Meghalaya, Nagaland, etc. as the route to the above place passes through the state of Assam"[67].

Assam shares border with China, Myanmar, Nepal, Bhutan and Bangladesh. The North East is connected to India by a small land bridge. The Bodos are one of the main indigenous tribes whose location can be found in the western region of Assam. As per the Census of 2001, the Bodos constituted around 5 percent of Assam's entire population[68].

There exists continuous conflict between the Bodos and the Muslim residents over the land ownership rights. In the 2008, the fighting between these two groups resulted in 55 deaths, more than 100 injuries and 200,000 people escaped to the refugee camps creating serious internal disturbances in Assam. The Bodos alleges that the undocumented Muslim migrants from Bangladesh are encroaching the land which is rightfully owned by them. The Muslim community, however, counters such allegation and observes that the accusation of the Bodo tribe is a false campaign to restrict their rights over land and to drive out the Muslims from the areas[69].

## Recent Violence and Instances of Internal Disturbances in Assam

Conflict and violent activities in Assam usually takes place between the Bodos and the Muslim migrants. In May 2012, a conflict between these two communities broke out when a signboard was allegedly removed from a Mosque by the Bodoland Territorial Council. The Council claimed that the Mosque was illegally occupying forest land. In protest, the All Bodoland Minority Student's Union, a local Muslim youth group called for the shutdown of the Kokraghar district. Subsequently, the confrontation between the Student's Union and the police led to many injuries[70].

Another tension between the Bodo and the Muslim migrants appeared in July 2012 in the same district of Kokrajhar. In that conflict four people shot one Muslim man and injured four others. After two weeks two men killed

Mohibul Islam, the founder and president of the All Bodoland Minority Student's Union, and Abdul Siddique Sheikh of the Muslim minority group. Subsequently four Bodo youths were killed in a Muslim dominated area[71].

The fighting that started in Kokrajhar spread to the neighbouring Dhubri districts where the groups torched hundreds of homes as a result of which around 400,000 people had to flee to the relief camps in the area[72]. Again in August of the same year, rumours of Muslim attacks on north eastern labour immigrants in south Indian cities was circulated through social media sites which led to a mass exodus from Bangalore and Chennai. So it created a situation of panic among both the parties requiring the security agencies to give extra effort to control the situation. The central government of India asserted that the rumour was designed to cause panic and spread fear among north east residents and hence blocked 250 websites and social networking sites, including Facebook, Twitter, Google, Youtube and fundamentalist Pakistani websites. It was revealed that Pakistan had a role to cause such panic and disturbances in India. The BBC reports that India has offered to share evidence with Pakistan that "the bulk of these messages, picture and evidences had their origin in Pakistan"[73].

It is to be noted that Bangladeshi Muslim migrants have a long history of conflict and confrontation with the general populace of Assam, besides confronting with the Bodos. It has always created many law and order problem which still continues in several forms. Conflicts, confrontation, burning of houses have been the general out come in such situation which is seriously destabilising the internal security of India's north east states.

The huge mass of irregular migrants does not belong to us. They cannot render absolute loyalty to our nation and their loyalty will always be suspected. Thousands of these migrants have been caught of manufacturing bombs, printing and distributing counterfeit currency notes and also aiding Kashmiri terrorists SIMI, ISI, and ISIS[74]. Former Army Chief of India Bipin Rawat observed that infiltration into Indian states is a pre planned strategy hatched by Pakistan and China and to keep the region boiling. Centuries ago Chanakya, the quintessential statesman had sent hundreds of his people to the neighbouring Vaishali to earn livelihood and operate as his informers. Similar thing is also happening in India. Most of these Bangladeshi infiltrators can easily be motivated to involve in anti-India activities and thereby creating serious problem for the safety and security of the Indian people. In the next chapter, certain measures undertaken at the government level have been analysed followed by some suggestions to check the ongoing problem.

## References


1. Bhattacharyya, Hiranya Kumar. (2018), *Operation Lebensraum: Illegal Migration From Bangladesh,* New Delhi: Bloomsbury Publishing India Pvt. Ltd, p.35-36.
2. *ibid.*, p. 54.
3. *ibid.*, pp. 54-55.
4. *ibid.*, p. 55.
5. *ibid.*, p. 55.
6. *ibid.*, pp.57-58.
7. *ibid.*, p. 55.
8. *ibid.*, p. 64.
9. *ibid*, p. 64.
10. *ibid.*, p. 64.
11. Das, J., Talukdar, D. (2016), "Socio-Economic and Political Consequence of Illegal Migration into Assam from Bangladesh", *Journal of Tourism & Hospitality,* Volume 5: 01.
12. Bhattacharyya, Hiranya Kumar. (2018), *Operation Lebensraum: Illegal Migration From Bangladesh,* New Delhi: Bloomsbury Publishing India Pvt. Ltd, p. 35, p.79.

13. *ibid.*, p. 79.

14. *ibid.*, pp. 85-86.

15. *ibid.*, p. 87.

16. Mishra, P.K. (2014), *Bangladesh Migrants: A Threat to India,* New Delhi: Gyan Publishing House, p.76.

17. *ibid.*, p.78.

18. Mishra, P.K. (2014), *Bangladesh Migrants: A Threat to India,* New Delhi: Gyan Publishing House, p.77.

19. Bhattacharyya, Hiranya Kumar. (2018), *Operation Lebensraum: Illegal Migration From Bangladesh,* New Delhi: Bloomsbury Publishing India Pvt. Ltd, p. 35, p.70.

20. *ibid.*, pp.71-72.

21. *ibid.*, p. 72.

22. *ibid.*, p.87.

23. *ibid.*, p.87.

24. *ibid.*, p.89.

25. *ibid.*, p.90.

26. *ibid.*, p.92.

27. Das, J., Talukdar, D. (2016), "Socio-Economic and Political Consequence of Illegal Migration into Assam from Bangladesh", *Journal of Tourism & Hospitality,* Volume 5: 01

28. The Times of India, August 2, 2018, Bhubaneswar, p. 05.

29. The Economics Time, August 03, 2018 p. 02

30. *ibid.*, p. 02.

31. The New Indian Express August, 05, 2018.

32. Bhattacharyya, Hiranya Kumar. (2018), *Operation Lebensraum: Illegal Migration From Bangladesh,* New Delhi: Bloomsbury Publishing India Pvt. Ltd, p. 35, p.79-80.

33. Assam: An Epitome of India, p.78

34. Demographic Aggression Against India, Balaji Rao p. 122.

35. The Voice of Assam published by Axom Sahitya Sabha, p. 14-15

36. Bhattacharyya, Hiranya Kumar. (2018), *Operation Lebensraum: Illegal Migration From Bangladesh,* New Delhi: Bloomsbury Publishing India Pvt. Ltd, p.32, 35.
37. *ibid.*, pp.32-33.
38. *ibid.*, p.33.
39. The Wonds of Indifference, Rajmohan Gandhi
40. Politics and Origin of the India-Bangladesh Border Fence, Rizwara Shamshad.
41. Behera, Subhakanta, *Trans-border Identities: A study on the impact of Bangladeshi and Nepali migration to India,* New Delhi, p.11
42. *ibid.*, p. 11.
43. Das, Pushpita (2016), *Illegal Migration from Bangladesh: Deportation, Border Fences and Work Permits,* New Delhi: Institute for Defence Studies and Analyses, p. 51.
44. Government of India, Annual Report 2014–15, *About 41.17 lakh people came from East Pakistan between 1946 and March 1958,* Ministry of Home Affairs, New Delhi, p.236.
45. Government of Assam, "Annexure 4– Infiltration and Deportation of Pakistanis", Directorate of Information of Information and Public Relations, Press Note No. 137, Shillong, July 27, 1965, in *White Paper on Foreigners' Issue*, Home and Political Department, Government of Assam, October 20, 2012, p. 56.
46. Mahanta, Prafulla Kumar (1986), *The Tussle between the Citizens and Foreigners in Assam*, New Delhi: Vikas, p. 86.
47. Upadhyaya, Priyankar (2006), "Securitization Matrix in South Asia: Bangladeshi Migrants as Enemy Alien", in, in Mely Caballero-Anthony, Ralf Emmers and Amitav Acharya (eds), *Non-traditional Security in Asia: Dilemmas in Securitisation*, Aldershot: Ashgate, p.25-27.
48. Bhasin, Avtar Singh (2004), *India–Bangladesh Relations,* Vol. 1, New Delhi: Geetika Publishers.
49. Sinha, S.K. (1998), "Report on Illegal Migration into Assam", [Online: web] Accessed 5 October 2018 URL: http://

www.satp.org/satporgtp/countries/india/states/assam/documents/papers/illegal_migration_in_assam.htm#PREVENTING INFILTRATION.

50. *Reforming National Security System*, Recommendation of the Group of Ministers, February 2001, p. 60.

51. *ibid.,*

52. Bhattacharyya, Hiranya Kumar. (2018), *Operation Lebensraum: Illegal Migration From Bangladesh,* New Delhi: Bloomsbury Publishing India Pvt. Ltd, p.45.

53. *ibid.,*

54. *ibid.,*

55. *ibid.*, pp.49

56. The Assam Tribune 2 May, 2016

57. Amar Axom 12 October 2014

58. Bhattacharyya, Hiranya Kumar. (2018), *Operation Lebensraum: Illegal Migration From Bangladesh,* New Delhi: Bloomsbury Publishing India Pvt. Ltd, p.52.

59. *ibid.*, p.53

60. *ibid.*, p.40

61. Mishra, P.K. (2014), *Bangladesh Migrants: A Threat to India,* New Delhi: Gyan Publishing House, p.33.

62. *ibid.*, p 34.

63. Dwivedi, Ashish. (2018), "Threat of illegal Bangladeshis to India's national security and political stability" [Online: web] Accessed 04 August 2019 URL:https://myvoice.opindia.com/2018/02/threat-of-illegal-bangladeshis-to-indias-national-security-and-political-stability/

64. Kumar, Anand. (2010), "Illegal Bangladeshi Migration to India: Impact on Internal Security" [Online: web] Accessed 02 August 2019 URL: http://www.pugwashindia.com.

65. Swain, A. (1996). "Displaceing the conflict: environmental destruction in Bangladesh and ethnic conflict in India" *Journal of Peace Research.*

66. Swain, A. (1996). The environmental trap: the Gange river division, Bangladeshi migration and conflicts in India. Uppsala (Sweden) Uppsala University Press.
67. file:///C:/Users/motag-ankitas/Downloads/Illegal%20MigrationNMF Sep%2020 13.doc#_ftn10
68. Bhattacharyya, Arpita, (2012) "Understanding the Historical Conflicts Behind Today's Violence in Assam" [Online: web] Accessed 08 July 2018 URL: https://www.americanprogress.org/
69. *ibid.,*
70. *ibid.,*
71. *ibid.,*
72. *ibid.,*
73. *ibid.,*
74. The New Indian Express 10th March 2018.

# 5

# Measures to Deal with the Problem of Irregular Migration

## Background

Due to several socio-political and economic challenges produced as a result of large scale population inflow in the form of irregular migration, there emerged serious demand among the general populace of Assam and some other affected section of people to securitize the issue of irregular Bangladeshi migration in India. Coming under the constant demand to consider the problem of irregular migration the government of India adopted certain measures to deal with the problem. The Government of India and the state Government of Assam adopted various measures which range from fencing of the India-Bangladesh long border, enactment of certain legislation which could protect the land rights of the indigenous population, discouraging the migrants to obtain land in Assam, setting up of certain tribunals to detect and deport the migrants. However, all these measures undertaken by the government of India and Assam government have not been able to meet the target i.e. to stop the continuous illegal entry to the country. Vested interests in India, vote-bank political interests of some political parties, non-cooperation of the indigenous people, constraint in fencing the long India-Bangladesh border are some major obstacles to give a full stop to the ongoing problem in Assam in particular and India in general. In this sphere it is pertinent to discuss about certain measures adopted by the government of India to meet the problem.

The Government of India, in its drive to stop the problem illegal infiltration from Bangladesh, has adopted several steps since the independence of the country in 1947. But the problem still exists and there is going on continuous inflow of population form its neighbour in various forms. Changes in government in Assam and at the Centre have also changed government's policies and decisions with regards to the migration problem. Even some governments in Assam went to the extent of supporting the illegal infiltration from Bangladesh only for their vote bank. The statement of Mr. Tarun Gogoi, the former Chief Minister of Assam can be a case in point who once said that migration problem in Assam is a non issue. However, with the growing dissatisfaction among the local Assamese against the Bangladeshi infiltration in to the state, the state government and the central government have given due attentions to the problem. Credit goes to Prime Minister Mrs. Indira Gandhi in taking serious steps to stop the problem. Subsequently Mr. Rajeev Gandhi also took the matter seriously when the Assam movement took place. P.V. Narshimha Rao also took various initiatives to deal with the problem in the last part of the 20$^{th}$ century. The BJP led NDA, before the general election of 2014, declared in its election campaign that if it comes to power then the infiltration problem in Assam will be solved. And as such, when the NDA came to power in 2014, it decided to implement the NRC under the direct observation of the Supreme Court of India in the year 2018. The final report of the NRC was published in 2019. In fact, the NRC is the most effective measure to solve the migration problem not only in Assam but also in the entire India. It provides mechanism to identify those people who are not the citizen of India but are living in the country since long years. Although the NRC is thought to be a proper mechanism to identify the Bangladeshi migrants, some intellectuals raise serious concern regarding its efficacy. At the same time the effectiveness of the NRC in detecting the irregular migrants in Assam should not be questioned as it was implemented under the direct supervision of the Supreme Court of India.

In the initial phase, the government of India, in its drive against continuous inflow of Bangladeshi migrants into Assam, decided to grant tenancy rights to the tribal in Assam which could protect their rights over land. Several legislations were made to grant occupancy rights to the native individuals of Assam and to deny the migrants to obtain land in that region. These steps served two basic purposes i.e. it watered over the growing dissatisfaction of the Assamese people due to encroachment of land by the foreigners and second discouraged the fresh migrants to cross the India-Bangladesh border as the prospect of obtaining land for their settlement became fewer.

## Measures

### Reserve the Land for the Tribal

In the year 1945, the tribal people of Assam under an organisation known as the Central Organisation of Assam started an agitation against the transfer of local land to the migrants of Bangladesh. In this sphere they wanted the government to stop the practice of land transfer in which the local administration played an important role. Their demand revolved round on eviction of all transferred land, remove the migrants from reserved forests and other areas and stop encouragement to the Bangladeshi migrants to come to India and finally redistribute the land to the land less tribal people of Assam[1].

After independence, the Government of India amended the Assam Land Revenue Regulation of 1886. In this sphere the Assam Land and Revenue Regulation Amendment Act, 1947 was passed. This act made the provision of creating Tribal belts and blocks i.e. village having more than 50 percent or more tribal populace and backward section of people were brought under the control of the tribal belts and blocks. In these blocks the tribal have right over land and hence no foreigners were allowed to encroach the land. This Act aimed at serving the purpose of discouraging the Bangladeshi migrants from land encroachment and consequently changing their migration decision to Assam. However in reality, the act could not produce the desired result and failed to address the problem of illegal infiltration. Earmarking the land for the tribal in inaccessible and infertile areas, protecting the welfare of the capitalists, tea plantations, land lords and non-tribal, who were residing over the tribal land etc, made the act ineffective to solve the problem. Consequently, the tribal people were deprived of land tenancy rights and forced to move to isolated and unfriendly areas of Assam.

Furthermore, the enactment of certain legislation by the Assam government to solve the problems of the people affected by floods and other natural calamities added to the woes of the tribal in Assam. One of these act known as the Assam Acquisition of Land for Flood Control and Prevention of Erosion Act of 1959 allowed the government of Assam to obtain land to relocate people displaced by floods and earth quakes. Thus the act benefited the Bengali migrants instead of the tribal because the migrants were staying in the low laying areas which were submerged during annual floods. These migrants were established in government-acquired land and were given tenancy or occupancy right. Subsequently, the act was challenged in the court and forced the government to repeal the act[2].

An analysis of the above fact makes it clear that the faulty government policy, political and bureaucratic apathy; vested interests could not solve the problem of Bangladeshi migration to Assam in the early years of independence of India.

## Detection and Deportation of the Migrants Through Legal Measures

### The Act of 1950:

In its drive to stop the illegal entry of the migrants from Bangladesh, the government of India adopted certain Action Plan which could detect the irregular migrants so as to deport them to their country of origin. Several tribunals were set up where complaints relating to illegal infiltration were referred to. The Government of India enacted an Act known as "Immigrants (Expulsion from Assam) Act of 1950, which came into effect from March 1, 1950. The act provided for the expulsion of any person who had been residing outside India but had entered India before or after the enactment of the Act and whose presence was detrimental to the interests of the general public or any section of the Scheduled Tribe"[3]. However, the act did not provide for expulsion of refugees who forcibly left Pakistan because of civil disturbances.

During 1950s, the process of detection and deportation of irregular migrants was not effective because Pakistan was still not considered as a foreign country. It was only on January 1957 that Section 2 (a) of the Foreigners Act of 1946 was amended which defined a Pakistani national as foreigner. So the "provisions of the Foreigners Act of 1946 were not applicable to irregular migrants from East Pakistan. Further, as the Pakistan nationals were not required to register themselves with the district magistrate if they entered to India through valid visas, there was no means available to trace Pakistani nationals who had entered India through legal process but did not return to his/her country after the expiry of visa duration"[4].

**Prevention of Infiltration of Foreigners Scheme:**

The population according to Census of 1961 made it clear that around 2,20,691 irregular migrant people had already penetrated to Assam. So the central government started a scheme known as "Prevention of Infiltration into India of Pakistani Nationals" (PIP) scheme in June 1962 which aimed at deterring the illegal infiltration of fresh migrants from East Pakistan. This scheme also made provision to keep a firm watch on the migrant settlement colonies in the border districts of the state of West Bengal, Assam, Tripura and Meghalaya. The police was empowered and vested the task of setting up surveillance posts in migrant settlement regions so that new migrants from East Pakistan can be identified and deported back. Such a step by the Union government proved highly productive which is evident from the fact that between 1961 and 1966, around 1,78,952 migrants were either deported or induced to leave Assam[5].

The scheme was, however, met with serious resistance. Due to serious opposition by some political parties and vested interests, who alleged that the government is harassing the genuine Indian Muslims in the name of detection and deportation of foreigners and the threat of Pakistan to bring the issue to the United Nations, the scheme was stopped. In other words, under serious political pressures the "Union government took away the powers to deport from the Deputy Commissioners (DCs) and the Superintendent of Police (SPs) and vested it in the Foreigner's Tribunals, which were established in September 1964"[6].

**Improvising the Scheme After 1971:**

The Government of India showed serious concern to the problem of irregular migration in India after Bangladesh emerged as a new state in 1971. An improvised scheme known as Prevention of Infiltration of Foreigners (PIF) was launched at that time. Also the Union government restored the power to evict Bangladeshis to the DCs and the SPs in 1976, because the illegal migration from across the border was not stopped even after the creation of Bangladesh. However, the government of India directed to DCs and SPs not to apprehend persons who had entered India before March 25, 1971. However, the improvised PIF Scheme was not able to achieve the desired goals due to temporary nature of the scheme, shortage of man power and infrastructure and severe political pressure against the scheme.

**Foreigner's Tribunal of 1964:**

The Government of India created the Foreigner's Tribunal under Clause 2 of the Foreigners (Tribunal) Order on September

23, 1964. The main function of the Tribunal was to decide the cases relating whether a person is foreigner or not. Thus, those person who were served notices to leave India, were given enough time to file petitions before the tribunals for the redress of their grievances. The alleged infiltrators, thus, got the opportunities to challenge the police case against them. Many tribunals were created in 1964 for this purpose and these were to some extent successful in deporting many migrants from the North East.

In fact, like the PIF plan, the Foreigner's Tribunal proved to be ineffective due to elaborate process of identification and deportation of irregular migrants, which also encouraged fresh migrants to come to India as they realised that the chances of being identified and deported is very less.

**The IMDT Act of 1983:**

The Foreigner's Tribunals in Assam set up under the Foreigners Act of 1946 was faced with serious opposition by political parties and some other groups. They alleged that the Act gives unbridle power to the police agency who misused the power to announce a person as foreigner (East Pakistani or Bangladeshi). Mainly some of the political parties, advocating the interests of the minority communities, alleged that legitimate Indian Muslims were stressed and compelled to leave the country in the name of deportation. To meet this opposition the Union government enacted the illegal migrants (Determination by Tribunals) IMDT Act, on December 25, 1983.

The main features of the IMDT Act were:

1. Provide for Tribunals to determine in a faire manner whether a person was an illegal migrant or not, so that the Government of India could expel him/her from the country.
2. Provide for an administrative committee which would examine the complaints under the Act, and reject complaints found to be frivolous.

3. Tribunals are to be set up to discuss the cases regarding suspected irregular migrants entering into India after March 24, 1971.

The earlier Foreigners Tribunal still continued to function along with the IMDT tribunals to dispose cases of suspected Bangladeshis who came before March 24, 1971.

***Shortcomings of the IMDT Act:***

The IMDT Act was not able to stop the problem of infiltration in Assam due to the following reasons:

1. A private person can lodge complain against someone about whom he had the information that the concerned person was an irregular migrant. However, the act provided "that both the complainant and the accused should reside under the same police station"[7].
2. The responsibility of providing that a person is an irregular migrant was on the complainant instead of the accused.

Thus the functioning of the IMDT Act remained sub optional. In 2005, the Supreme Court of India struck down the IMDT Act describing it as ultra vires and consequently all the IMDT tribunals ceased to function. Finally, all the pending cases were transferred to the existing Foreigner's Tribunals Act of 1964.

***Amendment of Foreigner's Tribunal Act of 1964:***

In 2012, the Foreigner's Tribunal Act of 1964 was revised. The amendment provided that all the petitions need to be heard and disposed within sixty days from its filing. The Foreigner's Tribunals have declared "38,000 persons as irregular Bangladeshi migrants in Assam since 1985"[8]. However, deportation of such population has been problematic as most of the migrant people are either fugitive or dead. The refusal of the Bangladeshi government to acknowledge these migrants as its citizens made the issue more problematic.

## Forcible Deportation

Although the tribunals were to some extent successful in detecting Bangladeshi migrants in Assam, it could not give a full stop to the foreign infiltration. In 1980s people from many quarters of India apprehended that migration from Bangladesh has assumed a new dimension with uncontrolled population infiltration taking place in India-Bangladesh border. Taking due consideration to the mounting dissatisfaction against irregular migration, Narshima Rao, the then Prime Minister of India, determined to adopt a strict measure which was known as "Operation Push Back" a most controversial measure to detect and deport the Bangladeshi infiltrators in India. The Action Plan aimed at detection, identification and deportation of the Bangladeshi migrants who had illegally crossed the border and settled in India[9].

However, Operation Push Back achieved little success due to the severe resentment of the Bangladeshi government which decried India's action as unilateral, illegal and unfortunate and alleged that India is by force pushing in Bengali speaking Muslims of India into Bangladesh. Within India the Chief Minister of West Bengal also showed indifferent attitude to the Union government's action and declared that it will not allow the central government to push back the alleged irregular migrants through the state's borer. Thus due to the pressure from both inside of the country as well as international pressure, the government of India was forced to suspend Operation Push Back in November 1992.

## Tightening of the India-Bangladesh Border

Tightening the international border in order to check the illegal entry of persons from Bangladesh was the most effective measure undertaken by the Government of India. Better management of the border, increasing the strength of the border guarding forces, construction of the fences and roads along the border, issuing identity cards to the border people were certain major efforts which have been undertaken to check the illegal or unauthorised movement of people from the neighbouring Bangladesh.

**Installing Better Surveillance System at the Border:**

Initially the Government of India did not perceive any security threat from cross border infiltration from Bangladesh side making the border poorly guarded. However, significant changes in the international security system forced India to revise its early stand on irregular infiltration of people from Bangladesh. Assam agitation, the Kargil war and several terrorist attacks in India were significant events which compelled the Indian policymakers for a tighter border control system. Of late, terrorist attacks in India emphasises the exigency of strict control of the border to stop the terrorists from moving in and out of the country.

For better surveillance of the border, the number of Border Outpost (BoPs) were increased. "From these BoPs the patrol parties are regularly dispatched to keep a vigil along the border to detect and deter illegal crossings. The patrol parties also collect tactical intelligence about the infiltrators and secret routes by studying the terrain of the border and interacting with the local people"[10].

The Government of India has also raised the number of BSF battalions who are deployed all along the border for a better border surveillance. Currently there are 80 battalions of BSF who are guarding the long India-Bangladesh international border. The water wing of the BSF has also played a key role in checking infiltration on the river which crosses the international border. These border guarding personnel are provided with electronic devices such as hand-held thermal imaginaries, night vision goggles and direction finders. Fast patrol boats are also in operation for inspection and interception along the riverine border[11].

**Cooperation between BSF & BGB to Check Illegal Infiltration:**

For better management of the India-Bangladesh border the Government of India has solicited the cooperation of the Bangladesh government. The BSF and the Border Guards of Bangladesh (BGB) have recognized many weak places along the international border which are used as a rout of infiltration into India. These border guarding forces also "conduct coordinated patrolling to keep a vigil along these secret stretches"[12]. Standard Operating Procedures (SOPs) to arrest the irregular migrants have been finalised between the two countries. These procedures have also been "revised in 2011 and again in February 2013. Under its provision, those infiltrators who are caught at the international border by the BSF are sent back immediately, and those who are arrested inside the country are deported to Bangladesh after taking legal action against them"[13].

**Fencing the India-Bangladesh Border:**

Fencing of the international border sharing with Bangladesh is another important measure undertaken by the Indian government to check the infiltration form Bangladesh. Fences acts as a physical barrier which not only checks the migrants coming to the country illegally but also checks many illegal activities such as drugs and cattle trafficking, arms smuggling, trafficking of women and many other associated crimes. Although, fencing the border has not given a full stop to the infiltration problem, it has increased the cost of such infiltration which has discouraged many clandestine entries. Fences made out of barbed wires, concrete walls, along with ditches, watch towers, sensors, cameras etc essentially slow down the movement of the infiltrators, thus making it easy for the security forces to apprehend them.

During the Assam movement, especially due to the wide spread violence unleashed during the agitation, the Indian government finally decided to build up fence along the

Bangladesh border. In April 1984, the central government decided to start constructing the fence which infuriated Bangladesh government leading to clashes at the border. The clashes between the border guards of "both the countries led to the death of few BSF personnel and members of the survey team and as a result, the construction of the fences had to be suspended temporarily"[14]. However, the Government of India again decided to fence the border despite the stiff resistance of the Bangladesh government.

The border fencing is not so easy due to unapproachable nature of the border in some places, problem in acquisition of land, non demarcated patches of the border and resistance from Bangladesh. Despite all the problems the borer fencing work is going on and is expected to be completed in near future. In fact the border fencing has been beneficial in checking infiltration and to stop several criminal activities.

## Certain Recommendations to Check the Problem of Irregular Migration from Bangladesh

### Border Management with the BSF Personnel:

Proper management of the India-Bangladesh border is a vital step not only to stop irregular migration but also to deal with the security threat to India due to large scale cross-border migration. Proper border management is possible only through coordination among political, legal, security, intelligence, diplomatic, administrative and economic agencies of the country. India-Bangladesh international border includes both maritime and land border which must be properly guarded by the security and border guarding forces of India. The BSF of India is now in charge of guarding the India-Bangladesh border. However, repeated withdrawal of the huge number of the BSF for interior security, counter insurgency as well as several other tasks is an unhealthy practice which makes the border vulnerable for illegal infiltration. Even the temporary withdrawal of the BSF personnel for other duties must not be resorted. Because the vacuum created due to such withdrawal is taken as advantage by the anti-socials who further helps the Bangladeshis to infiltrate into India[15]. Thus the BSF should be withdrawn from the border safety activity only under grave exceptional circumstances. At the same time the BSF must be given legal powers to prevent irregular migration, smuggling, infiltration and collection of intelligence.

**Conducting Motivational Training for Border Guarding Forces:**

In very few cases it has been reported in various news papers and other media regarding corrupt practices resorted by the border guarding forces of India. Some arrested infiltrators have also confessed about the role of some forces at the border facilitating their entry into India[16]. It is to be noted that, not all the border guarding personnel are corrupt but there are few black sheeps. Thus, in order to stop the happening of such unholy thing in the hands of our forces, motivational training should be conducted and they should be properly made aware of the disastrous consequences of cross border migration on the security of India. All these trainings should be organised before they are deployed at the border. Moreover, several in-service trainings are to be conducted for acquainting them with the current situation on the both side of the border. Steps should also be undertaken to establish a friendly relations and coordination between the border population and the BSF.

**Sealing of the India-Bangladesh Border Completely:**

"While the measures discussed above will help to tackle this problem, it is equally important to ensure that no fresh influx of immigrants takes place. Of the 4,096-kilometer border that the two countries share, 1,016 kilometres are riverine and 63 kilometres maritime. It is a porous border as it runs through rivers, ponds, agricultural fields, villages, and even houses where the entrance could be in one country and the back door in the other"[17].

Around 90 percent of the sealing of the India-Bangladesh border is complete and only few points are left behind. Due to the problem of land acquisition, around 101 kilometres border in West Bengal side is yet to be fenced. The Rajya Sabha was informed about this fact on 12th December 2012. Bangladesh has also changed its earlier position on fencing the border. At present the "Central Public Works Department (CPWD), National Buildings Construction Corporation (NBCC), National Projects Construction Corporation (NPCC)" and the Assam Public Works Department (PWD) etc are entrusted the work of constructing border roads, border fencing and installation of border floodlight[18].

Despite progress in the work, many instances of illegal infiltration of Bangladeshi people are taking place at the international border. So the fencing work must be completed as soon as possible and the border must be completely sealed. However, the quality of the border work also need to be taken into consideration[19].

**Spreading Awareness among the Border People:**

Vested interest in Assam always wants to create disturbances in the region so that their supremacy can be maintained by exploiting the emotion of the people of their own community. The fundamentalists and even some political parties devoid of patriotic sentiments seek to realise their objectives by dividing the society on communal line. Therefore general awareness needs to be created among the people of the affected areas so that they cannot be divided on communal lines. This initiative will not only create a situation of peace and harmony at the border state but also stop many organised crimes and violence and consequently avert a serious internal security threat to India.

**Strict Preventive Measures:**

At present the entire responsibility of identification and deportation of the irregular migrants in Assam and other regions of India lays in the hands some bureaucrats of the Ministry of Home Affair and the External Affair Ministry. It is therefore suggested that both the Central government and State government of Assam must come up with a strong determination to create an independent Central Immigration Control Authority[20] which would devise policies and action to prevent the illegal entry of Bangladeshi migrants.

**Protecting the Forest and Char Land:**

The migrants, after entering into India, generally eyes upon the forest and Char land of Assam. Even the land belonging to reserved forest and sanctuaries are very often encroached by them for their settlement. They clear the dense forest and start residing there which is seldom given any importance by the forest department and revenue department causing further encroachment of the forest land. As a remedy to the problem it can be suggested that the vacant chars and reserved forest areas should be properly sealed and brought under monthly supervision to ascertain that the land is not encroached. Eviction, if needed, is to be undertaken immediately with the proper guidelines.

In order to stop the practice of land encroachment in the forest and char, special task forces may be created which would include officers form police, revenue and forest department. Moreover, members of the civil society may also be included in the task force for better performances. The main responsibility of the task force is only to observe the land encroachment in the affected areas and it should not be overburdened to look after the infiltration. Another institution may be created which should control the infiltration at the border.

**Securitising the Issue of Irregular Migration at Political Level:**

At present there is lack of consensus among the political parties in India regarding the problem of Bangladeshi migration in the country. Many political parties in the country openly declares that there is no irregular Bangladeshi migrants in India. In West Bengal, the Trinamool Congress government headed by Mamata Banerjee has seriously shown her resentment to the central government when the later wanted to implement the National Register of Citizens in Assam in the year 2018 under the direction of the Supreme Court of India. Some political parties in India also openly criticise the process of identification of foreigners who have illegally entered and staying in the country. They decry the attempt as harassment to the minority community in India. However, the Bharatiya Janata Party (BJP) and the Asom Gana Parishad have considered the issue of Irregular migration as a security threat to India and are seemed to be determined to solve the problem through the implementation of NRC in Assam. The Home Minister of India in the month of November 2019 has already informed the country that NRC will be implemented throughout the country to identify illegal infiltrators in the country.

**Formulation of Strict Land Policy:**

Lack of strict land policy in Assam and other north east part of India helps the migrants to capture agricultural and other land through legal means. Many infiltrators from Bangladesh have already occupied vast amount of land in Assam with the help of corrupt officials. In this connection the instance of Zahidulla, a prominent jihadi activist and non citizen having acquired landed property and married a local girl can be the case in point. Thus there is need of bringing strict land policy in Assam. Before granting land right, proper verification must be done to ascertain the citizenship status of the buyer and all the lands should be confiscated forcibly which have been bought through corrupt means.

**Registration of the Villages in the Border Areas:**

Like the NRC there should be National Register of Village in the border areas of Assam and other north east. The unaccepted and unusual increase in the number of village in certain areas of Assam confirms the fact of continuous flow of new migrants in those areas. Thus in order to stop this thing all the villages must be brought under through scrutiny periodically and this task must be supervised by an impartial body. Moreover, no new villages must be allowed to surface in the forest, char and reserved sanctuaries or other government land. Political patronage to the development of the new villages must be checked[21].

**Amendment of the Citizenship Act:**

It can also be suggested that the Citizenship Act must be amended suitably so that children of Bangladeshi infiltrators do not get the right of citizenship because they were born in India/Assam/other north eastern states. Anybody born in Assam should be treated as Indian national only on the following ground:

- "If the person concerned satisfies the requirements as stipulated in Article 5 and 6 of the Indian Constitution.
- If the person's or his forefather's name is in the NRC of 1951.
- If his or her forefather's name is available in the ER of 1952 or 1971.
- If his or her forefather's mother tongue is either Assamese or any other language/dialect, spoken by the people of native origin in Assam"[22].

**Registration of Birth and Death:**

Lack proper mechanism to register the birth and death in Assam and other north east states has led to the growth of infiltrators there. The existing mechanism for birth and death registration is not sufficient to maintain a correct record. So an independent mechanism, free from all other works, should be created which should be assigned the task of birth and death registration in each quarter of a year. It should also be made mandatory for the people in all these states to register birth and death. Birth certificate must be a mandatory document in availing all the welfare benefits of the government, opening of a bank account, applying for driving license, passport, enumeration as voter, admission into primary school etc. It is through this practice we can get correct information on the growth of population in the north east.

**Banning the Infiltrators from Job Sectors:**

In the state of Assam it has been observed that the migrants are employed in various government, semi-government and private sectors. The contractors hiring these labourers do not verify their antecedents while giving them job. So it is suggested that the employment of the foreign labours not in possession of valid travel documents or visas must be banned. The contractors violating the rules must be booked under the law and they should be blacklisted. This practice will not only discourage the Bangladeshi infiltrators to illegally enter into India but also provide adequate employment opportunities to the youth of India with sound wage.

**Issue of Limited Period Work Permit:**

Issuance of limited-period work permit to the willing workers of Bangladesh after they sign an undertaking declaring their Bangladeshi antecedent will help India to give a statistics to the exact number of Bangladeshis in the country and accordingly help the country to devise policies to manage the issue. It will also discourage the migrants to disappear in the country due to the fear of deportation. However, after stability in their economic condition these migrants should be asked to leave or continue with a renewal of their work permit. This practice will be a significant step to stop the migrants in involving in criminal and terrorist activities in India[23].

**Verifying the Citizenship While Issuing License:**

In the state of Assam, one can find the Bangladeshi migrants working as rickshaw puller, driver and they also maintain a push cart to earn their livelihood. However, while issuing license for operating all these vehicle the authority do not verify the citizenship and other documents which attracts fresh migrants into Assam. In Guwahati alone, it has been reported that, more than 20,000 cycle-rickshaws are playing without license[24]. Thus it should be obligatory to verify the citizenship of all the applicants before issuance of license and the police must be empowered to seize all the vehicles operating without valid documents and licenses.

**Issue of Multi-purpose Identity Cards:**

Very often it becomes very difficult for the Indian agency to identify an infiltrator as these people can easily speak Bengali and share some cultural similarity with the Indian people. So for the identification of the irregular migrant there should be issuance of "multi-purpose national identity cards" to the genuine Indian citizens. However, while issuing these identity cards utmost care should be taken so that false people will not be given the opportunity to become Indian citizen.

**Confidence Building Initiatives at the Border Areas:**

Wining the confidence of the local people at the border areas and ensuring their participation in the border management can be a positive step to check infiltration of foreigners into India. For this purpose "Village Volunteer Force" may be created from among the people of the border areas. As these people reside at the border areas, they possess first-hand information on several areas and secret route which is used for infiltration. Moreover, development activities must be undertaken at the border areas so that they cannot be alienated. Facilities like proper roads, educational institutions, hospitals, electricity must be provided with sufficient quality. Development of social and economic structure in these areas will provide the unemployed youth jobs, so that they will not be involved in anti-social activities like drugs smuggling, arms smuggling, human and animal trafficking.

### Checking the ISI:

It is a well known fact that Pakistan's Inter Service Intelligence plays a key role in terrorist activities in India. Now the ISI eyes on these Bangladeshi infiltrators for terror recruitment and to cause further disturbances in India. So Pakistan must be pressurised by the international community to stop terror activities. Moreover, camps in Pakistan which trains the north-east Indian terrorists must be destroyed.

### Application of Modern Gadgets and Techniques:

It is very often alleged that the weapon system used by the border guarding force of India is not adequate to meet the new challenges. Modern gadgets and better weapons must be used and substitution of Indian Small Arms System (INSAS) rifle with more powerful rifle may be taken into consideration. Better sensor system, all weather Close Circuit Television (CCTV) cameras must be installed and the old machines should be replaced periodically.

### Coordination Between the BSF and the Border People:

Coordination between the border guarding forces and border population is a positive step to check illegal infiltration into India. In no circumstances there should be any differences of opinion among these two parties. The border population must be sensitised and encouraged to work as eyes and ears of the border guarding forces. Moreover, willing educated and fit youths must be recruited in all such border guarding forces as they know the terrain and language.

### Guarding the River Route:

It is to be noted that there are thousands of instances where the infiltrators enter into Indian territories through river route. Thus proper guarding of river through water patrol team should be prioritised. Moreover, the boat used by the Indian fisherman must be registered, it must use Indian flags and must have same colour as authorised to them. The registration work of the boats must be entrusted to the River Police Organisation (RPO)[25]. The Fisherman violating the international boundary on the river must be punished as per the laws. Furthermore, the boats, small or big, found without registration number and violating the general rules must be confiscated immediately.

**Supervision of the Working of Madrasas in Border Areas:**

It has been observed in few cases that, in the process of identification of Bangladeshi migrants some genuine Indian Muslims are harassed as they are asked to prove their citizenship. Thus proper care should be undertaken while dealing with all the cases and hence adequate protection must be provided to the Indigenous Muslim people in the border areas. If the Indian Muslims are taken into confidence and are free from even a small kind of harassment then it will be highly helpful to fight against the menace of Islamic militancy in the border areas. Moreover, the madrasas which are established for indoctrination of the innocent Muslim youths should be kept under proper observation. As these madrasas are used by the fundamentalists for terror recruitment there should be proper verification of its works and procedures and if any illegal things are noticed then it should be banned and closed immediately.

**Voluntary Registration Through Declaring Incentives for Migrants:**

Declaring a set of incentive for those irregular migrants who will voluntarily register themselves with a competent authority in India may be a positive step to identify the Bangladeshi migrants in India. The incentive may be in the form of granting work permit, permission to stay and work during the verification period or some monetary helps to those who declares themselves as migrants voluntarily. Similarly those migrants who do not declare themselves voluntarily but subsequently proved to be a migrant should be deprived of enjoying all the benefits given by the Government of India. They should also be debarred from getting work permit for hiding the fact[26].

## India-Bangladesh Bilateral Cooperation to Fight the Problem:

Since the problem of migration is an issue affecting the relations between India and Bangladesh, bilateral cooperation between them can be a concrete step in this direction. Denial of Bangladesh regarding the presence of its citizen in India must be fought by India with strong evidence and Bangladesh need to accept the fact first at the political level. The completion of the NRC in Assam has already confirmed the fact of presence of around 19 lakhs foreigners in India in which the Bangladeshi migrants constitute a major stock. Many political leaders in Bangladesh have already confessed that India has never raised the issue of Bangladeshi migration with her counterpart and this means that it is a non issue for the country. Thus in all the bilateral meetings the issue must be brought under the attention of the Bangladeshi government.

### Bilateral Agreement with the Bangladesh: Raising the Issue at the Bilateral Meeting

Bangladesh government has strictly denied the presence of any Bangladeshi citizen in India. Therefore it is not likely to accept those people who have, in reality, clandestinely entered into India. In fact, the Bangladesh government get the opportunity to deny the presence of its citizen due to the passive attitude of the government both at the centre and in Assam. The Bangladesh government has clearly stated that the Government of India has never raised the issue of irregular migration at any bilateral meeting between the countries. Seven Sister Post, an English daily once reported on 17th August 2012 that "Deputy High Commissioner of Bangladesh, Mahub Hassan Saleh, said that the illegal entry of citizen from his country into Assam has never been raised by the Indian government. I have been in New Delhi since the Awami League coalition-led government assume power in Dhaka and the issue of illegal migration has never been taken up by the Indian government"[27]. This instance clearly reflects the need of raising the issue in all the bilateral meetings with the Bangladesh government to find an amicable solution to the problem.

Global warming and climate change will cause more migrant to flow to India from the neighbouring Bangladesh. Sea level rise will result in the shrinking of many coastal areas in Bangladesh forcing them to move to India as the later is the most accessible area of destination. Therefore, the problem must be raised at the proper international meetings which are organised to discuss the problem of global warming and climate change. Bilateral agreement should also be conducted between India and Bangladesh for the extradition of irregular migrants, criminals and other anti social elements of both the countries. For this purpose legal tribunals may be constructed to complete the task. There is also the need to accept the problem by both the countries at the official level otherwise the problem cannot be solved rather it will be exacerbated in the coming days affecting the India-Bangladesh relations. At present the government of Bangladesh completely denies the presence of its citizen in India which is not good for friendly relations between the countries[28].

**Signing Treaty with Bangladesh for Repatriation of its Citizen:**

At present the Government of India has not signed any agreement regarding deportation of irregular Bangladeshi migrants from India. In the absence of any such treaty or agreement it is not possible to deport the infiltrators and the Government of Bangladesh will also not accept them as its own citizens. Thus some kind of agreement with Bangladesh is the only way to deport them.

### Socio-Economic Development in Bangladesh:

India should continue to assist Bangladesh in her socio-economic development. Income generation schemes must be adopted for the employment of the men and women in Bangladesh so that they will not see towards other country to earn their livelihood. Spread of education in Bangladesh must also be prioritised and the assistance of India is highly needed in such time. The Bangladesh government should also invite the expert from India in designing and implementing plans for the socio-economic development of the country. Moreover, curbing population growth in Bangladesh is to be prioritised as it has always put extra burden on the Bangladesh. In all the bilateral meeting with Bangladesh all these matters should be raised by India for a concrete action[29].

It is to be noted that development of free trade relations between India and Bangladesh will ensure the economic gain of both the countries. Free trade between both the countries will also give a full stop to many illegal import and export going on in the international border. Development of water route for commercial purpose will enable India to access Chittagong port of Bangladesh. It is believed that free trade between the countries will not only ensure their economic development but also reduce the migration of people from Bangladesh due to economic problem like poverty, employment and breakdown of their source of livelihood[30]. Bangladesh will be enormously benefitted if such economic relations are established.

### Convincing Bangladesh to Setup National Immigration Department:

Convincing Bangladesh to set up a national immigration department to study the problem of migration from the country will be a positive step which will act as an extra vigilance body at the border areas to stop migration from the country.

**Finding a Solution Through United Nations Organisation:**

As per the United Nations Convention, bilateral agreement must be conducted to fight against trafficking of person. India and Bangladesh being the members of the UNO should work together to implement such provision to stop trafficking of human at the India-Bangladesh border. Article 9 of the UN Convention says that, "State parties shall establish comprehensive policies, programmes and other measures to prevent and combat trafficking in persons and to protect victims of trafficking in persons, especially women and children, from re-victimisation". The International Court of Justice (ICJ) is another effective mechanism at the UNO where petition may be filed in case Bangladesh fails to stop its people going abroad illegally.

International organisations like the International Organisation for Migration (IOM) and United Nations High Commissioner for Refugees (UNHCR) are the best organisation which could help India to solve the migration problem. These organisations could also "play a significant role in assisting India and Bangladesh to resolve" [31]the problem.

**Convincing Bangladesh regarding the Economic Loss:**

It has been estimated that the Bangladeshi migrants found to be present in India send a huge sum of money to their own country. And this amount exceeds to crores of rupee every year. However, it is to be noted that the money is sent through illegal route by these migrants to their kin and kiths in Bangladesh. The middle men who are involved in the task of transferring money capture a large sum of that money and a few amounts are transferred. Thus it is suggested that Bangladesh should be convinced to recognise the presence of its citizens in India so that work permit can be given to these migrants and their money could be sent back to their own country through proper channel[32].

## Identification of Irregular Bangladeshi Migrants Through Implementation of the National Register of Citizens (NRC):

On the direction of the Supreme Court of India in 2013, the Central Government of India decided to start the long awaited National Register of Citizens (NRC) in Assam. The first NRC in Assam was done in 1951 to register the genuine citizen of the country in the citizen's list. Due to the continuous flow of population from the neighbouring East Bengal which became Bangladesh later, people in Assam were, since long, demanding for the identification and deportation of the infiltrators from the state as the infiltrators were changing the demography, economy and culture of Assam. The All Assam Students Union took the lead to start a state wide agitation with the demand to detect and deport the illegal migrants from Assam and to save the Assamese to become a minority in their own region. The state wide agitation started in 1979 and continued till 1985 with the signing of the Assam Accord in 1985. The party to the Accord were the Central government, the State government of Assam and the AASU. Initially the central government tried to crush the movement and there was police firing and lathi charge on the agitating students in the Nagaon College, but in 1980 central leaders like Indira Gandhi, Shankardayal Singh started talking with the students union to find out a solution. Even Atal Bihari Vajpayee who became the Prime Minister of India later on went to Assam to meet with the students in their AASU office. Prafulla Kumar Mahanta the former Assam Chief Minister and a signatory of the Assam Accord in 1985 in his interview to the Economic Times on August, 2019 said that 855 people were martyred in the six year long agitation[33]. The Assam movement was signed in the year 1985 and the then Prime Minister of India Mr. Rajeev Gandhi admitted the fact of the presence of foreigners in Assam. The cut off date for the detection and deportation of the migrants was fixed at 1971.

The Rajeev Gandhi government, however, could not take

concrete action to identify and deport the foreigners in Assam as per the Assam Accord. The Bengali settlers and the Muslims in Assam expressed serious anger over the process of identification of the foreigners. Although the survey to identify the migrants began in November 1985 it angered the Muslim and Bengali community living in Assam. These people were of the opinion that, as we were living and working in the state since long why the government is asking us to prove our identity. While Mr Rajeev Gandhi did not directly order to stop the process but he maintained that it (identification and deportation process) should be done properly which slowed down the entire process.

Coming to the twenty first century, in the 2014 general election the BJP declared in its election campaign to identify and deport all the foreigners from Assam. Subsequently the party came to power and under the direction and supervision of the Supreme Court of India the Union government started the implementation of the NRC in Assam. The first draft of NRC was published in 30th July 2018 where the names of 40,00,000 (Forty Lakh) people were missing from the citizen's register. Although, the publication of the NRC was a draft report, leaving opportunities for those whose names are missing from the list to file claim and objection to prove their Indian citizenship, it created serious resentment from many political parties mainly from the TMC of West Bengal. The chief minister of West Bengal alleged that the central government is trying to harass the genuine Indian Muslims. She also threatened the Centre not play with fire in the name of NRC. Despite such hues and cries the final report of the NRC was published in 31st August, 2019 where the names of around 19,00,000 (Nineteen Lakh) people in Assam was missing. Mentioning the statement of the state NRC coordinator Mr. Prateek Hajela, the Times of India reported on 1st Septemer 2019 that "The NRC exercise is a mammoth exercise involving around 52,000 state government officials. All decisions of inclusion and exclusion were taken by these statutory officers. The entire update process has been meticulously carried out in an objective and transparent manner"[34]. It is not that all the migrants have asked to leave the country but they have been given the opportunities to go the Tribunals to file petition and to prove their Indian citizenship with proper documents. The foreigner's tribunal have the authority either to declare person foreigner or overrule the NRC findings and declare a person as Indian citizen. The Home Minister of India Mr. Amit Shah informed the Rajya Sabha on 20th November 2019 that the NRC will be implemented in all states throughout India. However, some political parties and organisations in Assam were not satisfied with final NRC report who called the final NRC a flawed exercise. Assam finance minister Himanta Biswa Sarma said, "The name of many Indian citizens, who migrated from Bangladesh as refugees prior to 25th March 1971, have not been included in the NRC because the authorities refused to accept their refugees certificates...Many names got included because of manipulation of legacy data, which many alleged"[35]. Dissatisfied with low exclusion numbers, the AASU, a prime stakeholder in the NRC case in the Supreme Court said that it will move to the Supreme Court for rectifying the errors. Further the AASU said that the number of Bangladeshis in Assam is more than the 40 lakh people who were excluded in the draft NRC published in the 2018.

The Ministry of External Affairs clarified that those people whose names are missing in the final NRC published in 31st August 2019, are not "state less" and will continue to enjoy all the rights as before till they exhausted all the remedies available under the law. The state government of Assam has set up hundreds of tribunals where the proposed foreigners can file petition to prove their citizenship[36]. The response of the MEA came after the UN High Commission on Refugees (UNHCR) made a statement that the NRC may render a large number of people stateless. The statement further cleared that "while India has sovereign right and authority to try to establish who is an Indian national and who is not, UNHCR urges the government to take steps that mitigate the risk of any individual being left stateless as a result of the NRC update exercise in Assam or similar processes that may take place in other states in India". The MEA of India's spokesperson Mr. Raveesh Kumar made it clear that those excluded can appeal for inclusion before foreigners' tribunal till 31st December 2019. Thereafter any one still aggrieved by any decision of being excluded will have the right to approach the High Court of Assam and then the Supreme Court[37]. The Government of India also stated that no action shall be initiated against any person so long as the final decision of the Court does not come. So there is nothing to be worried for genuine Indian citizens about the NRC report.

Documents to be produced to be enrolled in the NRC of Assam:

1. Land documents like Registered Sale Deed, records of land rights up to March 24, 1971 (midnight).
2. Permanent Residential Certificate issued up to March 24, 1971 (midnight).
3. Passport Issued by the Government of India up to March 24, 1971.
4. "Life Insurance Corporation of India Policy (LIC) of relevant period up to March 24, 1971 (midnight).
5. Any license/certificate issued by government authority of relevant period i.e. up to March 24, 1971 (midnight).
6. Document showing service/employment under Government/ Public Sector undertaking up to March 24, 1971 (midnight).
7. Bank/Post Office Accounts of relevant periods i.e. up to March 24, 1971 (midnight).
8. Birth Certificates issued by the competent authority up to March 24, 1971 (midnight).
9. Educational Certificate issued by Board/Universities up to March 24, 1971 (midnight).

10. Records/process pertaining to court up to March 24, 1971 (midnight) provided they are part of a processing in a judicial or Revenue Court".

(Source: The New Indian Express, 2nd September 2019, Monday, p.9)

Although the mechanism of NRC aimed at identifying the infiltrators in Assam in particular, it does not seem to be realising the desired objectives. The Government of India itself is confused regarding the application of the process. Views of ministers in the government differs from one another regarding the number infiltrators in India. Initially the NRC also excluded the name of 40 lakhs people in Assam from the draft NRC, now it comes to 19 lakhs. So doubt arises regarding the proper application of the process to identify who are the citizens and who are not i.e. foreigners. There are many instances where the names of parents come in the NRC list leaving their children from the final list. So it gives enough chances to doubt the functioning of the NRC in Assam. In spite all these facts it cannot be denied that if the NRC is carried out properly then it can be a suitable mechanism to identify the infiltrators in Assam and from other states of India.

## References

1. Saikia, Arupjyoti. (2014), *A Century of Protests: Peasant Politics in Assam since 1900*, Oxon: Routledge.
2. Das, Pushpita. (2016), *Illegal Migration from Bangladesh: Deportation, Border Fences and Work Permits,* New Delhi: Institute for Defence Studies and Analyses, p. 60.
3. Section 2 of the Immigrants (Expulsion from Assam) Act, 1950, Act No. 10 of 1950, March 1, 1950, [Online: web] Accessed 5 November 2019 URL: http://indiankanoon.org/doc/1523917/, accessed on February 9, 2015.
4. Das, Pushpita. (2016), *Illegal Migration from Bangladesh: Deportation, Border Fences and Work Permits,* New Delhi: Institute for Defence Studies and Analyses, p. 61.

5. *White Paper on Foreigners' Issue*, n. 6, p. 8.

6. Das, Pushpita. (2016), *Illegal Migration from Bangladesh: Deportation, Border Fences and Work Permits,* New Delhi: Institute for Defence Studies and Analyses, p. 62.

7. *White Paper on Foreigners' Issue*, n. 6, p. 16.

8. Das, Pushpita. (2016), *Illegal Migration from Bangladesh: Deportation, Border Fences and Work Permits,* New Delhi: Institute for Defence Studies and Analyses, p. 67.

9. Ramachandran, Sujata. (2003), "Operation Pushback': Sangh Parivar, State, Slums, and Surreptitious Bangladeshis in New Delhi", *Economic and Political Weekly,* Vol. 38, No. 7: 638.

10. "Annexure X–Internal Note Prepared by the Home Ministry, Government of India in March 1992", n. 13, p. 258.

11. "Floating Outposts Give BSF Strategic Edge", *Business Standard,* February 23, 2015, Hasnabad, [Online: web] Accessed 5 November 2019 URL: http://www.business-standard.com/article/news-ians/floatingoutposts- give-bsf-strategic-edge-115022300623_1.html.

12. "B'desh No Longer has Rebel Training Camps", *The Times of India*, Shillong, February 6, 2015, [Online: web] Accessed 2 October 2019 URL: http://timesofindia.indiatimes.com/city/guwahati/Bdesh-no-longerhas- rebel-training-camps/articleshow/46136666.

13. "Illegal Migrants", Unstarred Question No. 6211, Lok Sabha, May 5, 2015, [Online: web] Accessed 2 July 2019 URL: http://mha1.nic.in/par2013/par2015-pdfs/ls-050515/6211.pdf.

14. Ghosh, Partha S. (1989), *Cooperation and Conflict in South Asia,* Delhi: Manohar, 1989, p. 85.

15. Bhattacharyya, Hiranya Kumar. (2018), *Operation Lebensraum: Illegal Migration From Bangladesh,* New Delhi: Bloomsbury Publishing India Pvt. Ltd, p.188.

16. *Ibid* p.188

17. Tripathi, Sanjeev. (2019), *Illegal Immigration From Bangladesh to India: Toward a Comprehensive Solution* [Online: web]

Accessed 15 May 2018, URL: http://carnegieindia.org/2016/06/29/illegal-immigration-from-banglades-to-india-towards-comprehensive-solution-pub-63931.

18. Mishra, P.K. (2014), *Bangladesh Migrants: A Threat to India,* New Delhi: Gyan Publishing House.
19. Bhattacharyya, Hiranya Kumar. (2018), *Operation Lebensraum: Illegal Migration From Bangladesh,* New Delhi: Bloomsbury Publishing India Pvt. Ltd, p.188.
20. *ibid* p., 179.
21. *ibid* p., 186.
22. *ibid* p., 190.
23. Sarma, Madhumita. (2015), *A Study of Migration from Bangladesh to Assam, India and Its Impact,* Ph.D Thesis, p.210, Adelaide, SA 5005, Australia: The University of Adelaide.
24. Bhattacharyya, Hiranya Kumar. (2018), *Operation Lebensraum: Illegal Migration From Bangladesh,* New Delhi: Bloomsbury Publishing India Pvt. Ltd., p.191.
25. Bhattacharyya, Hiranya Kumar. (2018), *Operation Lebensraum: Illegal Migration From Bangladesh,* New Delhi: Bloomsbury Publishing India Pvt. Ltd, p.189.
26. Tripathi, Sanjeev. (2019), *Illegal Immigration From Bangladesh to India: Toward a Comprehensive Solution* [Online: web] Accessed 15 May 2018, URL: http://carnegieindia.org/2016/06/29/illegal-immigration-from-banglades-to-india-towards-comprehensive-solution-pub-63931
27. Bhattacharyya, Hiranya Kumar. (2018), *Operation Lebensraum: Illegal Migration From Bangladesh,* New Delhi: Bloomsbury Publishing India Pvt. Ltd, p.198.
28. Sarma, Madhumita. (2015), *A Study of Migration from Bangladesh to Assam, India and Its Impact,* Ph.D Thesis, p.209, Adelaide, SA 5005, Australia: The University of Adelaide.
29. Bhattacharyya, Hiranya Kumar. (2018), *Operation Lebensraum: Illegal Migration From Bangladesh,* New Delhi: Bloomsbury Publishing India Pvt. Ltd, p. 183.

30. Sarma, Madhumita. (2015), *A Study of Migration from Bangladesh to Assam, India and Its Impact*, Ph.D Thesis, p.209-210, Adelaide, SA 5005, Australia: The University of Adelaide.
31. Tripathi, Sanjeev. (2019), *Illegal Immigration From Bangladesh to India: Toward a Comprehensive Solution* [Online: web] Accessed 15 May 2018, URL: http://carnegieindia.org/2016/06/29/illegal-immigration-from-banglades-to-india-towards-comprehensive-solution-pub-63931
32. Bhattacharjee, Joyeeta. (2014), *India: Resolving the Bangladesh Immigration Issue* [Online: web] Accessed 15 May 2018, URL: https://thediplomat.com/
33. The Economic Times 2nd August, 2018.
34. The Times of India 1st September 2019 Sunday, p. 01.
35. The Times of India 1st September 2019 Sunday, p. 01.
36. The New Indian Express, 02nd September 2019, Monday, p. 09.
37. The Times of India 2nd September, 2019, Monday, p. 06.

# Conclusion

In fact, irregular Bangladeshis' migration to India is the biggest security threat which India is facing today. As per various studies, it has been found that the number of Bangladeshi people, who are staying illegally in India, could be around 15-20 millions. Since the British rule, movement of the people from East Bengal to Assam is noticed. Subsequently such population movement continued unabated after the creation of Pakistan in 1947. The emergence of Bangladesh as an independent state, after its separation from Pakistan in 1971 did not stop the population movement from Bangladesh to India. The Assam Movement of 1979-1985 was a serious voice against such illegal infiltration to the state. Bangladeshis have not only infiltrated to Assam but also their presence can be found in almost all states of India now. The presences of the Bangladeshi nationals have been found in the states like Delhi, Mumbai, Gujarat, Tamil Nadu, Odisha and many others. Although some political parties in West Bengal deny the presence of any Bangladeshi nationals, the fact gives a different picture. There may be some political interests behind such denial. The Minister of Home Affairs of the Centre in the winter secession of the Rajya Sabha has informed the house that the NRC will be implemented in all the states of India so that the foreign citizens, illegally staying in India, will be identified. The latest NRC in Assam has confirmed the presence of around 19 lakh foreigners in Assam in which most of them are Bangladeshi nationals. The famous Assam accord set 24th March 1971 as the deadline to become a citizen of India. In other words, those who have entered India after 24th March 1971 will be identified and deported. However, the lack of political interests to implement the NRC in Assam facilitated further infiltration into Assam from Bangladesh. Many politicians, researchers and academicians have already observed in their research works that irregular infiltration at India-Bangladesh border is still going on. Even today the migrants have devised new strategies to enter India. The New Indian Express once reported that the Bangladeshi nationals are entering India through legal means but subsequently they have not returned and have been vanished in India.

The causes behind such infiltration are varied and a multiple of push and pull factors work behind it. Refugees or the people who leave a country for reason of political persecution or state atrocities or religious intolerance can be accepted in India on humanitarian ground. However, the economic migrants who leave a country for reason of devastation of their source of livelihood due to various factors cannot be accepted in a country which is already under stress to provide its own people a qualitative life. India is already under population pressure and an additional population stress due to illegal infiltration of Bangladeshis is making the situation more precarious. The scarcity of living places due to rapid population increase caused by polygamous marriage practice and absence of birth control awareness among the Bangladeshis has made Bangladesh a densely populated country. At present Bangladesh is encountered with the double problem i.e. uncontrolled population growth and scarcity of land for inhabitation of its people. Adding to this, the problem of climate change and global warming has made the situation more unstable. Floods and cyclones in Bangladesh have devastated the source of livelihoods of millions of Bangladeshis and it has consequently pushed them into abysmal poverty. Moreover, various climate studies confirms that sea level rise in Bangladesh will result in the submergence of many coastal cities in the country. And as such the consequence will be the search for new source of livelihood and better place for inhabitation. The cities and big towns in Bangladesh are already overpopulated which cannot adjust an additional population in that. Thus the consequences will be the movement towards neighbouring India which, they consider, as the most accessible and safe place for them. Illiteracy, poverty and backwardness make them vulnerable to become irregular migrants in India who infiltrate India crossing the international border. The cost of hiring a visa and the ignorance to fulfil the legal norms forces them to opt for shortcut ways and illegal channels to enter into India. No doubt, religious persecution has forced millions of Hindus to leave the country who have settled in India but there number is less in comparison to the economic migrants, most of whom belong to Muslim community. Since Bangladesh is an Islamic state there is no question of religious atrocities against its own community and hence there is no reason for leaving the country due to religious atrocities or state persecution. Most of them are economic migrants who comes to India due to economic reasons i.e. better economic opportunity, better health and education facilities etc. Thus their entry to India is not a response to protect their life from violence and atrocities but to obtain a better source of livelihood.

India is a developing country with a high number of populations. The country is in the process of achieving the status of a developed country and it still fights with many challenges like poverty, backwardness, and health challenges. Terrorism, Naxalite problem, crimes against women and children, gender inequality etc are some important challenges with which India is fighting. Among the several challenges, irregular Bangladeshis' migration problem in India is the biggest threat to the safety and security of the country. The problem is very old and specifically the Indian state of Assam is the worst sufferer of the problem. These economic and irregular migrants have already brought about many changes in the social, economic, political and demographic structure of Assam. Many scholars, academicians, government officials, and ministers have expressed serious concern to such changes which Assam is facing due to uncontrolled population infiltration from Bangladesh. Even the Supreme Court of India has directed the Government of India to check the problem in Assam. The implementation of the NRC in the year 2018-2019 in Assam is the case in point. The population in Assam, mainly from Muslim community has registered a significant growth which has been highlighted in this research work. The India-Bangladesh border inside India is marked with the growth of numerous villages making the border over populated. The then Governor of Assam S.K. Sinha in his report to the then President of India has mentioned about the demographic invasion of Assam due to the uncontrolled and illegal entry of Bangladeshi nationals to the state. Vote bank politics, presence of vested interests in India have helped these migrants to settle in Assam. It is to be noted that if such infiltration continues then a day will come when the local and original Assamese will be reduced to a minority in their own region.

Encroachment of government land and land belonging to reserved forest and sanctuaries, by these foreign nationals, has been a general phenomenon in Assam. The forest cover of Assam has been declined at a rapid rate. After their arrival, these migrants clear the forests, occupy the forest land and settle their villages. They also help in the further migration of their relatives and subsequently form groups to face any resistance to them by the local Assamese. In fact, Assam is facing serious environmental stress due to the reduction of its forest cover day by day. The decline of forest covers in Assam in various years have been discussed in this research work. In spite of all these unwholesome developments in Assam, some political parties and the state government turned a deaf ear to the problem for many decades which encouraged further migration of Bangladeshis to the state.

Competition over jobs, changes in the wage structures, and large scale unemployment of local Assamese youths are some notable changes noticed in the state. The migrants are very hard working and are ready to work even in odd hour. As they are ready to work in relatively low wages, it has seriously changed the wage structure there. The job contractors also give preference to the Bangladeshi workers to the local Assamese due to the readiness of the former to work with low wage. The unskilled and semiskilled job sectors in Assam is now flooded with Bangladeshi workers who have taken away jobs from the local youths which causes serious irritation among the youths of Assam. It also cannot be denied that the lure for a salaried job, the easy going attitude of most of the Assamese youth have paved the way for sleeping of jobs into the hands of these migrants. If a local Assamese produce one crop in one season in his land then a Bangladeshi produces three crops in one year in the same agricultural land. In spite of all these facts it cannot be denied that the Bangladeshi migrants have significantly changed the economic structure of Assam which causes serious resistance against them by the local people.

India is a developing country, the country is yet to fulfil the rising expectation of its increasing population and an additional population pressure in the form of migrants of Bangladesh is, no doubt, creating pressure on the economy of the country. It is the first and foremost duty of any responsible government to fulfil the needs of its own people. Humanitarian consideration can be made only to the refugees who flee a country due to religious persecution or state atrocities against them. However, the economic migrant, who come to a country for economic reason and consequently put pressure on the economy, demography and security of the receiving country, is objectionable. To be more specific, the Bangladeshi Muslim migrants do not come under the refugees who come to India not due to religious persecution but for economic reason i.e. to escape from gruelling poverty and economic backwardness back in their home.

The first hypothesis i.e. socio-economic, political and environmental problems in Bangladesh has endangered the life and livelihood of most of its population and consequently forced them to migrate towards India, has been tested in chapter three of this research work and is proved valid.

The second hypothesis i.e. ongoing changes in the climate condition in Bangladesh will exacerbate irregular migration to India is also experimented in the chapter three of this research work and is found valid. Economic backwardness, poverty, unemployment, over population and population growth, scarcity of land for inhabitation and agriculture, illiteracy, weak health care system, poor educational facilities are some major problems with which Bangladesh is still grappling with. Bangladesh is one of the most densely populated country and the situation is worsening due to uncontrolled population growth caused by early marriage and polygamous marriage practice. Agriculture is one of the major sources of livelihood for a majority section of people in the country. However, reduction in agricultural land due to various environmental hazards and over population has negatively affected their life and livelihood. Absence of any alternative source of livelihood for its people and the inadequate place in town and cities forces them to take migration decision. Many compulsions back home which cannot be repaired, shapes their migration decisions. Millions of people in Bangladesh, who left their home for other country like India, have witnessed these entire problems which cannot be repaired at all in home. Moreover, Bangladesh is prone to various environmental hazards due to its geographical location. The country has witnessed the worst kind of natural disasters in the past which has destroyed the houses, agriculture and other source of livelihood of millions of its population. It has also been predicted that the pattern of environmental hazards in Bangladesh is going to be multiplied in the coming days due to the rapid changes in earth's climate condition. Many coastal areas in the country are under serious threat of submergence in the sea water as the sea water is rising due to melting of glaciers. The agriculture, which is a major source of livelihood for millions of people in the country, will be severely affected, consequently threatening their life and livelihood. Thus the affected people will have no other option but to search for a safe place which could assure them of safety in their life livelihood. Migration within Bangladesh is not a suitable option for them as the cities and towns in the country are already overpopulated which cannot adjust an additional population. In fact climate change is going to add their suffering in future. Many studies have confirmed that, in future India will face the large number of climate refugees from Bangladesh. And as such, climate change and global warming is going to add in the number of irregular Bangladeshi migrants who are already present in India. Although, in the present research no intensive studies have been made to study the climate induced migration from Bangladesh, but little attempts have been made to study the link between climate change and Bangladeshis' migration to India. Thus climate-induced migration from Bangladesh is going to shape India's future security which needs to be studied.

The third hypothesis i.e. irregular Bangladeshis' migrants are serious security threats for India is tested and proved in chapter four of this research. The securitisation of irregular Bangladeshi migrants in India can be traced back to the late 1970s when the All Assam Student's Union started a state wide agitation to identify and deport the irregular migrants most of whom belong to Bangladeshi nationals who have illegally settled in Assam. Thereafter, the political parties at the centre and state started politicising the issue to exploit general sentiments for vote bank. Thousand of agitating people were dead and there were also instances of other law and order problem in Assam which awakened the central government to interfere on the issue. The process of securitisation of the irregular Bangladeshis' migration started with the signing of the famous Assam Accord in 1985. The accord provided for the identification and deportation of all the foreigners who are illegally staying in Assam.

It is to be noted that all the Bangladeshi migrants are not criminals or terrorists or are involved in anti-India activities. The gross generalisation of the issue is dangerous and may lead to serious human rights violation. Therefore utmost care is to be taken to deal with the problem because the migrants, in spite of their irregular status in India, possess right to life and dignity. Most of the migrants coming from Bangladesh are illiterate and excessively poor. Their culture and way of life also significantly differ from the general populace of Assam. Lack of education and poverty on the part of these migrants makes them vulnerable to fall prey in the hand of the anti-India networks working in Assam and other parts of India. To be more specific, the Muslim fundamentalist elements in Assam try to establish close relations with the migrants. The religious similarities also help them to establish such relationships. Many instances of terrorist recruitment from the migrants stock have been unearthed by the security agencies of India. The enormous growth of madrasas in border area plays a key role in the indoctrination of the Muslim youths. Moreover, the hidden intention of Pakistan to convert Assam into a Muslim majority region cannot be ignored. The Inter Service Intelligence (ISI) of Pakistan and Director General of Foreign Intelligence (DGFI) of Bangladesh are trying to build Greater Islamic Bangladesh which would include whole of present Bangladesh, West Bengal, Assam, Tripura, Meghalaya and parts of Bihar, Jharkhand and Odisha. Thus the sovereignty and integrity of India is under threat due to illegal population infiltration from Bangladesh.

In this work, the security implications of irregular migration from Bangladesh have been thoroughly analysed and it is found that Assam is facing serious problem in the sphere of economy, culture and demography. Moreover, the internal and external security of Assam and other states of India is under serious threat due to such infiltration. The sovereign right of India is seriously compromised when a foreigner illegally infiltrate into the country and subsequently vanished. Their (the migrants) chances of falling prey in the hands of the anti-Indian and terrorist network has forced India to think seriously about the problem. If India will skip the problem under the pressure of the international human rights body then its sovereignty and integrity will be under serious danger. Thus the problem needs coordinated efforts involving both India and Bangladesh to reach to an agreeable solution. India has never ignored the human rights of foreign nationals which is evident when the country gave shelter to Dalai Lama in Dharmasala of Himachal Pradesh. Again the refugees who fled Pakistan, Bangladesh and Afghanistan due to religious discrimination and atrocities on religious ground have been given food, shelter and have been treated properly with due importance of their human rights in India. Thus the international community cannot underestimate India's role in accepting the ill fated people who suffered religious biased back in their home countries. At the same time it is also the supreme duty and Constitutional obligation on the part of India to protect the country's sovereignty and integrity at any cost and it cannot be compromised at all.

How the internal security of Assam is threatened has also been investigated in the present research. Various instances of conflicts and violence between the local tribal in Assam and the migrants are analysed. Group attacks, burning of the houses, ill treatment to women and girls and even instances bombing is found to be noticed in Assam. Most of the criminal activities such as drugs and animal trafficking, smuggling of weapons, circulation of fake currencies are certain activities which are given effects by some of these irregular migrants in Assam. Thus at present the Bangladeshi migration problem has become a serious headache for India due to its multifarious security threat for the country.

The fourth hypothesis i.e. inter-state or regional cooperation involving India and Bangladesh government could be a positive step to address the emerging security problem, has been tested and proved valid in chapter five of the present research work. Irregular migration is a problem which involves both India and Bangladesh and hence requires coordinated efforts by both the countries for a better solution. The denial of Bangladesh government regarding the presence of her nationals in India is making the problem more complicated. Thus India has to come with adequate evidence to prove the presence of Bangladeshi nationals on her soil. The government of Bangladesh also need to be convinced in such a way that it will accept the gravity of the problem affecting both the country. Bilateral cooperation between the governments of both the countries is the need of the time. The government of India need to raise the problem at all the regional and international meeting with Bangladesh because the Bangladesh government has frequently stated that India has never raised the issue of irregular migration with Bangladesh.

Poor economic condition, unemployment, poverty of people, weak health care system and population growth are the main causes of irregular migration from Bangladesh to India. In this connection India should help Bangladesh in its infrastructural development. Industrialisation with the help of India can be a positive step in employment generation and poverty eradication in Bangladesh. Experts from India in the fields of economics, education, and health care system can play a significant role in giving their valuable suggestions for the development of Bangladesh.

Again, the fencing of entire India-Bangladesh border is possible only with the proper cooperation of the Bangladesh government. There should also be proper coordination with the Border Security Force of India and Border Guards of Bangladesh. Intelligence must be shared for their mutual benefits. Fundamentalist elements, working in Bangladesh must be brought to justice and all the anti-India activities inside Bangladesh must be stopped and this can be possible with the proper coordination between both the countries. In today's world no country can go to war or aggression for achieving its national interests and hence mutual dialogues and discussions are suitable option for solving various issues affecting them. And in this connection India and Bangladesh are no exception and whatever problems that exist between them can be solved only through bilateral dialogue and mutual cooperation.

In this work efforts have been made to interlink irregular Bangladeshis' migration and the security of Assam in particular and India in general. Although various studies have conducted to unearth the link between migration and security but few researches has been done to analyse the security implications of irregular Bangladeshis' migration for India. Moreover, this research also studies the factors like climate change which forces and will continue to force millions of Bangladeshis to infiltrate into India. In other words, this research also briefly studies the future pattern of migration from Bangladesh to the neighbouring India in which very few research have been done. Thus the present research attempts to fill the existing gaps.

Keeping in view all these findings as obtained from this research, it can now be said that Irregular Migration from Bangladesh is the biggest security threat which India is facing today. Hence the national security discourse of India needs to include irregular migration as a threat to the security of the country. Also there is need for proper securitisation of the problem, rising above its mere politicisation. There is also the need to devote more energies and resources to solve the problem. It is to be kept always in mind that while securitising the issue of irregular Bangladeshi migration problem, the human rights of the migrants always needs to be considered. All the migrants are not criminals or cherish any criminal intentions; there are large numbers of children, women, girls, poor, weak and old people in the migrant stock who are the most vulnerable section and they are not criminals. Therefore there is the necessity to reasonably deal with the problem so that the safety of these people will not be compromised at all along with the protection of the sovereignty and security of India.

At present India is not faced with the problem like war or aggression, but is now confronted with various new and more dangerous problems which not only threatens it's institutions but also the entire human being living in it. Thus the new and non-traditional security threats are shaping India's present security environment. It is to be noted that the non-traditional security threats are more dangerous than the traditional military security threats. In other words, the nature and intensity of these soft security threats are more catastrophic, sudden and can cause unimaginable destruction for a country. In this situation, scholars, academicians and other research organisations need to undertake scientific study of the problem and can provide their findings for resolving the century long problem which India is still facing. Irregular Bangladeshis' migration to India is a problem which needs emergency and extraordinary efforts because we cannot wait till the problem assumes an overwhelming character. Thus before the problem starts threatening the core interests of India i.e. it's sovereignty and integrity we should adopt strict measures to solve the problem.

# Index

**J**



**K**



**L**



**M**

## P



## R

**W**



**Z**